Playing

TO GET

Smart

Elizabeth Jones

Renatta M. Cooper

TEACHERS
COLLEGE
PRESS

Teachers College
Columbia University
New York and London

Published by Teachers College Press, 1234 Amsterdam Avenue, New York, NY 10027

The authors wishes to express gratitude to the following for granting permission to excerpt from these works. All works are copyrighted by their publisher, unless noted: S. Cronin & C. Sosa Massó (2003), *Soy Bilingüe*, Seattle, The Center for Linguistic and Cultural Democracy; M. Donaldson (1978), *Children's Minds*, New York, W. W. Norton [copyrighted by author]; J. Gonzalez-Mena (1993), *Multicultural Issues in Child Care*, Mountain View, CA, Mayfield/The McGraw-Hill Companies; E. Jones & J. Nimmo (1999, *Young Children*), "Collaboration, Conflict & Change"; K. Moore (Schmidt) (1998), *Extending Experience*, unpublished master's thesis, Pacific Oaks College, Pasadena, CA [copyrighted by author]; V. G. Paley (1988), *Bad Guys Don't Have Birthdays: Fantasy Play at Four*, University of Chicago; L. M. Silko (1977), *Ceremony*, New York, Viking Penguin, a division of Penguin Group (USA) Inc.

Library of Congress Cataloging-in-Publication Data

Jones, Elizabeth, 1930–
    Playing to get smart / Elizabeth Jones, Renatta M. Cooper.
      p. cm. — (Early childhood education series)
    Includes bibliographical references and index.
    ISBN 0-8077-4616-9 (pbk. : alk. paper)
      1. Play.   2. Early childhood education.   3. Cognition in children.
    I. Cooper, Renatta M.   II. Title.   III. Early childhood education series
    (Teachers College Press)

  HQ782.J65 2005
  155.4'18—dc22

                                                        2005051048

ISBN-13: 978-0-8077-4616-5   ISBN-10: 0-8077-4616-9 (paper)

Printed on acid-free paper

Manufactured in the United States of America

13 12   11   10 09 8 7 6   8 7 6 5 4 3 2 1

Contents

Prologue

To survive and thrive in a changing world, people need to think creatively. Social-problem solving is a necessary life skill. Representing experience in symbolic ways, including through language and literacy, is a necessary life skill. Play is the most basic way children develop these skills. Teachers of young children need to provide opportunities for quality play within the learning environment. Teacher education and staff development need to support teachers in valuing play for themselves and children and in educating parents on the benefits of play.

This vision of early schooling contradicts political pressures for standardized education. Schooling is basically a conserving activity, designed to socialize the young into the status quo. It ensures that most children of poverty won't become smart; if they were smart, they'd start demanding more opportunities. Such demands discomfit those who benefit from power and privilege—including power over the educational system. Universal standards measured by testing guarantee winners and losers.

We are teachers who learned our trade in an era in which early childhood programs could get away with lots of play time, because it was generally assumed that the early years aren't important. But things have changed. Perhaps early childhood professionals, including us, have worked too hard to convince the public that the early years are crucial not only to social-emotional development but also to preparation for school and even to brain development. Our advocacy for the importance of early childhood education has backfired, supported by the hard scientists who are always seen as the most believable folks around. (They play hardball and are adept at capturing federal dollars.)

Children are born ready to learn, and they learn continually, as all early childhood educators and parents know. However, policy makers now mean something different when they speak of "ready to learn" as a goal. Because everyone's basic model of schooling is direct teaching, children as young as 2 are being drilled in word recognition, and kindergartens have replaced blocks with worksheets. Children too active or too egocentric to sit still for long periods of time are labeled as not ready to learn and advised to wait a year. The blame is placed on their parents, their communities, and their cultures. And on their teachers, some of the best of whom are leaving school systems that deny them freedom to teach creatively.

If we pay attention to the children, we rediscover that they are not all alike, nor should they become so. Young children are active learners, eager to make sense of their world. And fortunately, they're not good at sitting still and listening. In self-defense, then, almost everybody responsible for the care of the very young lets them play, at least some of the time. Play is what young children do best. Skillful young players can do it for a long time, without interrupting adults to complain, in words or actions, of boredom. It's through play that young children get smart.

PLAYING TO GET SMART

playing (pla'ing), v.i., Choosing what to do, doing it, and enjoying it.
smart (smart), adj., Optimistic and creative in the face of the
        unknown.

These aren't the definitions you'll find in the dictionary—although *smart* does get characterized by *Webster's* as "vigorously active; alert and dexterous; quick in learning." And among the many dictionary descriptors of *play* are "to move or function freely; to pretend; to do for amusement, profit or edification."

These definitions are ours, playfully invented to reflect the circumstances in which we find early childhood education at the beginning of the 21st century. The United Nations Declaration of the Rights of the Child includes the child's right to play along with the rights to be fed, clothed, sheltered, and educated:

The child shall have full opportunity for play and recreation, which should be directed to the same purposes as education . . . to enable him to develop his abilities, his individual judgment, and his sense of moral and social responsibility, and to become a useful member of society. (United Nations, 1959)

Play is *autotelic* behavior; it's self-chosen and self-directed. All healthy young children are highly motivated learners in search of play opportunities.

STAGES IN PLAY

Young children from birth to age 8 progress through a series of developmental stages in which play becomes increasingly complex. Each stage builds on the skills and knowledge gained in the one before.

Exploration

From infancy to age 2 or so, babies are sensorimotor *explorers* of their world so-new-and-all. They play first with body parts they haven't yet figured out are theirs—hands, mouths, and whole bodies become tools for discovery. Cheerfully messing about with whatever they encounter, the youngest children practice noise making and locomotion and cause and effect. They play with all the materials they encounter: What's this? What does it do? What can I do with it? They are building the base of physical knowledge on which all later learning depends. And they learn to play with other people.

Babies are good at the beginnings of thinking—curiosity. Curiosity is easily stamped out for the sake of approval.

Sociodramatic Play

Three-to-5-year-olds are beginning to acquire logical knowledge: What are the connections between all these things? And all these people? They are practicing *representation*—the many ways in which human beings pretend that something is something else. Gesture, talk, dramatization, image making, and writing are all tools for personal reflection and interpersonal communication. "I sitting at table," "I'm the mama, and you gotta eat your dinner," "I drawed a pizza," and the wobbly letters "E D" added to her drawing by 4-year-old Edie are all playful communications in which something is standing for something else—words for action, pretend roles for real ones, drawings for objects, squiggles on paper for spoken words. Young children are creating and practicing in play the skills they will need to become literate—decoders of squiggles on paper.

Investigation

Six-to-8-year-olds are becoming increasingly purposeful *investigators* of the natural and human phenomena outside and inside classrooms. As "serious players" (Wasserman, 2000), they can be challenged to think critically both in their spontaneous activity and in teacher-planned, open-ended activities. How does this work? Could we do it another way? What are all the ways it could be done? Learning is shared, and represented, both in group conversation and in meaningful squiggles on paper—drawing and writing.

At each stage, playful learning is *active*. As players grow older, it becomes increasingly reflective—thoughtful—as well. Young human beings are members of a species of meaning makers; all their lives they will play with ideas. They will tell stories and construct images to represent what happened to them today and yesterday and last year, and to create visions of what might happen tomorrow and in the future.

WHERE IS THIS BOOK GOING?

This book is about thinking—what it's for, why it's dangerous, how to support it in both children and adults. Play demands *divergent thinking*: What are all the ways we could do this? If we do this, what will happen?

While you're reading this book, see if you can find a good idea you'd like to try. And look, too, for an idea you wouldn't try, and talk to someone about why you wouldn't.

We've designed the book as a game of *assumptions* that we're inviting you to play with us. The next chapter will introduce the rules of the game. The rest of the chapters will be full of stories.

1

Playing with Assumptions

ALL of us—we as writers, you as readers of this book—engage in play with ideas. This process begins in early childhood, though young children act it out with their bodies and materials rather than relying on words and the thoughts they represent. Adults are good at words, which they combine into *assumptions* about the world and how it works and what's of value. Our nature and nurture—our temperament, our experiences, and what we have been systematically taught—have combined to steer each of us toward accepting some assumptions as true and good and rejecting other assumptions as bad, or at least misguided. Our daily behaviors as early childhood educators reflect our assumptions, whether we acknowledge them or not.

We grow, as thinking persons and as teachers, through continual play with possibilities. Learning happens when we experience disequilibrium—when something doesn't fit our established patterns. As we question, revise, and retest our ideas, we engage in lifelong learning.

Because we authors think it is desirable, especially for teachers, whose job is full of the unexpected, to engage in conscious reflection and dialogue on what we believe and what we do, this book is designed as play with assumptions. Since we're the initiators of the play, we get to define the content and set the rules. (Play *does* have rules. They just differ from the rules of established games like soccer and chess, in that they haven't been preinvented by somebody else. Players make up the rules as they go along, within the structure of their broader understanding of *what is play*.)

Here is the list of assumptions we have chosen to think about:

- Complexity is more interesting than simplicity. Up to the level of everyone's ability to cope, the more diverse an environment, the more learning will occur.
- It is more efficient to build action on intrinsic motivation (what people want to do) than on rewards and punishments.
- Democracy is a better bet than dictatorship. Sharing power is safer than trying to hang on to it all. To liberate is wiser, in the long run, than to domesticate.
- Becoming consciously bicultural is more powerful than either assimilating or maintaining separateness.

1

- Giving things their right name is a better idea than keeping names secret.
- *We* can outwit *Them*.
- *We* can practice caring for *Them*. And we should, because peace-making is safer (though less exciting) than making war.

BASIC PREMISE: BEING SMART IS DESIRABLE IN A CHANGING WORLD

We are assuming that young children will become smarter under these conditions:

- If they are offered a complex environment with many possibilities to choose from.
- If they are offered practice in choosing—finding out what they want/care about.
- If they are treated democratically and expected to help take responsibility for the democratic community.
- If they are in an inclusive environment in which they are able to experience both the comfort of a solid identity and the challenges of being an outsider.
- If they are helped to name their experiences, gaining access to the power of representation.
- If they are helped to be strategic in confronting power.
- If they develop empathy.

The smart person:

- Knows what she wants.
- Can strategize on how to get it.
- Has empathy for others and their wants.
- Is skillful in negotiating win/win solutions with others.

Intellectual and moral autonomy should be the aim of education (Kamii, 1982; Piaget, 1973). Intelligence is both intellectual and social/emotional. Morality is about relationships with others.

ENJOYING DISEQUILIBRIUM

Smart, we believe, is being optimistic and creative in the face of the unknown. Every time we get our world figured out, something previously unknown comes along to confuse us again. When that happens in our home or workplace, we have to do something about it. A book, however, is only a book; it invites you to participate, but it doesn't make you take action. You can even put this book down right now if you think you're not going to like it—unless, of course, you're reading it because someone in power, your teacher, assigned it in a class you have to pass. Students who "don't get it" but pass their classes anyway have learned skills of faking it, and you will find advice for "outwitting Them" later in this book, to add to your already considerable knowledge.

Everyone's working assumptions reflect the theories they have "in their bones," constructed from all their life experiences. JoeAnn Dugger explained this to the instructional aides enrolled in her in-service class in child development:

I pointed out to them that each of them had a theory about children; the only difference was that they had never written theirs down and gotten famous. So we were going to learn about the famous theories written about in the book, and then each person could add to or change their theory as they observed children and saw how it checked out with the others. Or write theirs and become famous. (Jones, 1983, p. 53)

If your experiences have been different from ours, you may disagree with our ideas. That's fine; our goal is to create disequilibrium and provoke critical thinking. Hang in there. These are our working assumptions at this moment in history. We are offering them as provocations for mutual play.

EMBRACING CONTRARIES

As you have noticed by now, the game is stacked. We have stated our preferences as assumptions, rather than posing them as questions (Which is better, liberation or domestication?). As authors, we have the floor and hope you'll pay attention, but not just shake your head yes or no. We want you to play with us.

Smart grownups play with ideas. Both doubting (saying no) and believing (saying yes) serve them as play strategies; both are learned through diligent practice, beginning in childhood. ("I am so the mommy!" "You're not my friend." "Oh, you're meowing—here, kitty kitty.") Budding scientists are taught to doubt—to think critically rather than to accept dogma from any source. In Western civilization "the Renaissance was in effect the victory of the free marketplace of ideas. We no longer empower any institution to keep reprehensible ideas out of circulation" (Elbow, 1986,

p. 283). Both democracy and modern science grew out of the commitment to question whatever others take for granted—to play the doubting game.

Reading this book, you may doubt us all you like. But we'd also like to invite you to try something different and probably harder: the believing game. It's a game of pretend, something early childhood educators know a lot about. Here's how to play it in response to our assumptions.

If you find that you agree with us, this will be too reassuring a reading experience. So we invite you to make it more of a challenge by trying to put yourself in the shoes of a reader who finds that she actively disagrees. Why might she? What's not true in what we've written?

If you disagree with us, don't just indulge in arguing. Instead, reserve judgment long enough to ask yourself, How could these authors believe these things? What is it in their temperament, experience, and cultural background that could possibly lead them to think that children who are smart (by their definition) are desirable companions and citizens?

What's the point of this game?

Imagining another person's perspective on things requires the suspension of reality (what I really believe) in order to pretend. (This is what someone else believes. Could I, if I tried hard?) In the diverse world we live in, we keep encountering people who don't believe what we believe. We can sneer at them, or fight them, or pretend they're invisible (until they step on our toes). Or we can accept the challenge to "embrace contraries" (Elbow, 1986).

[The Queen said,] "Let's consider your age, to begin with—how old are you?"

"I'm seven and half, exactly."

"You needn't say 'exactly,'" the Queen remarked. "I can believe it without that. Now I'll give *you* something to believe. I'm just one hundred and one, five months, and a day."

"I can't believe *that!*" said Alice.

"Can't you?" the Queen said in a pitying tone. "Try again; draw a long breath and shut your eyes."

Alice laughed. "There's no use trying," she said; "one *can't* believe impossible things."

"I dare say you haven't had much practice," said the Queen. "When I was your age I always did it for half an hour a day. Why, sometimes I've believed as many as six impossible things before breakfast." (Carroll, 1979, p. 213)

Alice in Wonderland/Through the Looking Glass is a nonsense story that many generations of children and adults have found remarkably memorable. It plays with complex ideas. It surprises and puzzles us and makes us laugh. It startles us into attention. Thinking about play, we mustn't get too serious.

Which side of a leopard has the most spots?
The outside.

CONNECTED KNOWING

Practicing the believing game makes *connected knowing* possible (Belenky, Clinchy, Goldberger, & Tarule, 1986):

Connected knowers develop procedures for gaining access to other people's knowledge. At the heart of these procedures is the capacity for empathy.
    Connected knowers know that they can only approximate other people's experiences and so can gain only limited access to their knowledge. But insofar as possible, they must act as connected rather than separate selves, seeing the other not in their own terms but in the other's terms. (p. 113)

Doubting supports competition; believing supports connection and seeks consensus. It creates "the challenge to care" (Noddings, 1992) for others rather than to beat them at their own game. We ask children to believe that other children feel pain, just as they do. (That's hard to imagine, when you're 2.) We remind adults that the monsters children imagine are really scary and worth crying over. We ask teachers to have empathy for the job of being a parent, and parents to understand why the teacher doesn't always attend to their child's expressed needs. We ask children, as they grow, to share responsibility for making the classroom community work. We hope adults can build on all these understandings in sharing responsibility for making the world work—through compassion, consensus building, and reconciliation.

What does every tarantula wish he had?
A hairy godmother.

There will be many stories in this book—to wake you up, to give you pleasure, to tickle your brain. Here are a couple of our efforts to practice believing.

PLAYING THE BELIEVING GAME

Janet Gonzalez-Mena's little book *Multicultural Issues in Child Care* (1993) provides me (Betty) with lots of stories that challenge me to doubt and to believe. Under "Varying Perspectives on Early Self-Feeding," she describes just what I, with a new graduate degree in child development, practiced years ago with my own very young children:

The experts in this country agree that it is important to encourage babies to take part in the feeding process. . . . no matter how much mess results. "Not only does this support a feeling of independence, but it also permits him to develop greater skill in using his hands." Other experts advise leniency about letting children *mess around* with their food, and indeed even see it as *gaining sensory experiences.* (p. 32)

And I remember fondly the moment when, in a friend's kitchen, I handed my hungry 9-month-old a dish of applesauce but no spoon, because she couldn't yet manage a spoon. The 11-year-old daughter of the house took in this scene and said hastily, "I think I'll leave!" and she did.

And then Janet turns the tables by convincingly presenting all the reasons why this view is not to be believed.

In some cultures, food is revered and is never considered a plaything. . . . Anyone who has experienced severe food shortages may be horrified at the thought of playing with food. [Further, in some households] the priority is on preventing rather than cleaning up messes. Prevention means spoon-feeding the baby. (pp. 32–33)

Janet, who is my friend of many years and more deeply sensitive than I to cultural issues, goes on to ask me to practice believing that my views may not be the last word:

The opposing values of independence versus interdependence often lie behind conflicts that involve self-help skills, like self-feeding. I remember some of the Hispanic parents I used to work with who spoon-fed their children far beyond the age that I considered reasonable. I was trying to make their children independent through early self-help skills; they had different ideas. They were less concerned about children helping themselves than they were about teaching them to help others. By feeding them, they were modeling the behavior they were trying to teach. The goal was interdependence.

If you see little reason to stand alone (on their own two feet, as the expression goes) but lots of reasons for them to experience and value relationships, you may be very willing to let self-help skills come much later. You may see a value in one person being dependent on another. The point is mutual dependence. . . .

Interdependency is a lifelong condition, one that relates to permanent attachment with one's family or one's people, something that is highly valued in some cultures. (p. 33)

When I was reading Janet's book for the first time, I had recently been present at a Head Start graduation. The ceremony was followed by a picnic lunch, where I was shocked to see an African-American grandmother spoon-feeding her just-graduated 5-year-old. He can feed himself! was my reaction. But I have realized, with Janet's help, that that's not the point. By his gracious acceptance of his grandmother's feeding, he was respecting her love and her right to care for him. He was also keeping his nice clothes nice, Renatta reminds me. Believing doesn't come easy, but I improve with practice.

Last year I (Renatta) was visiting a kindergarten class in which the teacher said to me about a boy in her class, "Alejandro can't do anything!" Never having met a 5-year-old who can't do anything, I couldn't believe *that*. So I pursued my doubts by watching Alejandro. His teacher was wrong; he could do lots of things, but I did notice that he lacked skills in handling blocks, or even in walking carefully past precarious block structures. Two very competent airport builders were, in fact, doing their best to keep him away.

"Tell me about Alejandro's family," I said quietly to the teacher. "He's the fourth child and the only boy," she said. Clearly, Alejandro has lots of reasons to be graciously interdependent, but kindergarten blocks may be a new experience. I stepped, with relatively little guilt, out of my observer role. "Alejandro, *ven acá*," I said. "Can you help me build a tower with these blocks?" He was gracious, even with me, a stranger; this child has been raised in an atmosphere of trust.

And I taught him, just as I would a 2-year-old, about the balancing of blocks to keep a tower standing tall. That's not a necessary home skill, but it's a basic kindergarten skill. Alejandro at 5 has two settings in which to learn, home and school. He is learning two languages, two kinds of relationships (with loving family and with standards-conscious teacher), and many skills suitable to either or both settings, home and school. How much overlap will he discover between his two worlds? Do school and home respect each other? The process of acculturation/biculturation is a challenging one. But if he is fortunate, he will learn to become effectively bicultural, in order to thrive in the complex city in which he lives.

IMAGINING AS A SKILL

Digressing into stories is something you will catch us doing throughout this book. Why?

*I will tell you something about
stories,*

[*he said*]
They aren't just entertainment.
Don't be fooled,
They are all we have, you see,
all we have to fight off
illness and death.
(Silko, 1977)

Stories are what we remember. Stories are true, in the context in which they are told. Many stories depend on the *suspension of disbelief*—on accepting the context of "Once upon a time . . . in a land far away . . . " If we can do that, we have *imagination* as a powerful tool for rethinking the world as it might be. Much human knowledge has its roots in someone's "believing as many as six impossible things before breakfast."

Even Harvard medical students, we learn from Robert Coles in his book *The Call of Stories* (1989), need to learn more than techniques to make us well. Using fiction to introduce moral and ethical inquiry, Coles writes, "I have found myself constantly learning new ways of interpreting those fictions—taught by my undergraduate and medical students" (p. vii).

To accept, and practice, any of the assumptions we have used to organize this book, you need to be a good *imaginer*, open to risk taking and the pleasure of not knowing what will happen. If you are an early childhood educator, this is a game in which you are probably more practiced than most people. Teachers and caregivers of the very young mostly play the believing game. They admire children's play; they don't correct wrong answers; they acknowledge the child's world as a separate and interesting place. They may watch and listen more than they talk. The comment attributed to more than one evaluator visiting a classroom, "I'll come back when you're teaching," is therefore a silly comment in a developmentally appropriate preschool.

Beyond preschool, teachers haven't been permitted to behave this way—to watch children learning through self-initiated activity. Instead, they're supposed to doubt wrong answers, to question, to correct, to assert authority over children's knowledge as well as their behavior. Many teachers don't get beyond that expectation. Not only is it prescribed, but they also enjoy the power of being right, and the certainty of doing what's right keeps them safe from temptation.

That behavior, we suggest, doesn't go far toward helping children (or teachers) get smart. Children need adult models of playful, engaged learning. But here's Seymour Sarason's (1972) observation, which we think is even truer now than when he wrote it:

I have spent thousands of hours in schools and one of the first things I sensed was that the longer a person had been a teacher the less excited, or alive, or stimulated he seemed to be about his role. It was not that they were uninterested, or felt that what they were doing was unimportant, or that they were not being helpful to their students, but simply that being a teacher was on the boring side.

... what would be inexplicable would be if things turned out otherwise, because schools are not created to foster the intellectual and professional growth of teachers. (p. 124)

We believe that the intellectual and professional growth of teachers depends on *their* playing to get smart—as children do, but in grownup ways. We're inviting you to play with us here.

If this were 5 centuries ago, we'd be trying a different set of assumptions on you. These are assumptions for our times. We are asking you to join us in thinking through their implications for child-rearing and education in a rapidly changing, diverse, and often violent world. Try believing them—just as a game, of course. See where these assumptions take you, as we discuss them one by one in this book.

What did the octopus say to his date?
I want to hold your hand, hand, hand, hand, hand, hand, hand.

2

Enjoying Complexity

Assumption: **Complexity is more interesting than simplicity. Up to the level of everyone's ability to cope, the more diverse an environment, the more learning will occur.**

Why did the whale cross the ocean?
To get to the other tide.

Why did the chicken cross the playground?
To get to the other slide.

Why didn't the hen cross the road?
It was feeling a little chicken.

WE enjoy jokes because they surprise us. They break the established pattern; they tickle our fancy, just as tickling a baby surprises and delights.

Human beings are pattern makers. They move things around to improve on the randomness of natural order. They move ideas around inside their heads, and in conversation with friends and colleagues. They move word meanings around; until we started collecting jokes for this book, from the children's page of our local paper, we hadn't realized that most kids' riddles are puns. Patterning is an important form of play.

Natural disasters undo people's carefully invented patterns. All over the world, earthquakes are among the disasters that come along. Some children respond at the level of avoidance; a preschool teacher told me (Renatta) that they were having peanut butter for snack when a quake hit and that Damon has refused to eat peanut butter ever since. Perhaps this is his magical way of ensuring that there will be no more earthquakes.

Some teachers are more capable than others in guiding children to the resolution of powerful events through active and engaged play. Laurie Read has described her children's play after a big California quake:

The 1989 Bay Area earthquake was a truly memorable thing that happened in all our lives. It was played and talked about over and over.

Nick and John (whose dads are fireman and policeman respectively) had been building fire houses and jails that were crashed by a "bad guy." On the day after the quake they constructed a road remarkably similar to the Cypress structure (where the freeway fell) and alternately crashed and rebuilt all morning.

That afternoon Garth got out the stacking pegs. He was stacking them just high enough to be unstable. He would shake them very gently at first, then violently. When I asked him to explain his game, he said he was playing aftershock. The aftershocks "were the little ones, then comes the BIG ONE" at which time the pegs would fly off the board and go all over the place.

We did some experimenting with the sizes of buildings—2 peg buildings were less likely to fall, we decided, than 5 or 6 peg buildings—especially during aftershocks. I asked Garth how tall his house was (stories) and he said it was 2 stories tall. He decided his house should be safe since it wasn't as tall as 5 pegs. . . .

Tanya was on the fire engine. I was rocking it back and forth for the amusement of Jerry. Tanya popped up, "It's the earthquake time!" She laughed and shook it harder. I laughingly suggested she drop and cover. She immediately buried her head into the crook of her arm (while still balancing on top of the fire engine). Then she told me to do the same. We traded "drop and covers" until she had three other children alternately shaking and covering too. (Reynolds & Jones, 1997, p. 106)

Laurie's program included a wide age range of children, from 2 to 6, and she has written eloquently about the learnings that happen across this range. As the bigger children take charge of their fears by building and destroying and building again, 2-year-old Jerry wanders by. And he's little, so we have to be nice to him. Multiage grouping provides a rich context for complex thinking:

The only real problem seems to come with blocks and toddlers wading through the older kids' constructions. We now yell "earthquake" when towers fall, and of course the only sensible thing to do after an earthquake is dry your tears and rebuild. (As one of the kindergartners puts it, "That's what we get for living in California!"—so philosophical, my bunch!) (Read, 1993, p. 16)

What do cows give after an earthquake?
Milkshakes.

CONVERGENT THINKING

Convergent thinking simplifies. It invites focused attention toward the right answer, the revealed truth, the peak of skillful achievement.

In convergent thinking, we learn and practice rules invented by someone else: spelling, vocabulary, basketball, and so on. If the rules are complicated and we're ready for the challenge of the game (and therefore likely to win it most of the time), then playing games with rules is both educational and recreational. The system and its limits are known; the challenge is to beat it through practice that increases one's skill and knowledge. Practically anything can become a game for someone: rock climbing, crossword puzzles, math worksheets, poker, and even taking tests. Convergent thinking yields right answers. And sometimes world records.

Safety rules are based on convergent thinking too. Where earthquakes (here we go again) are a fact of life, earthquake drill is a prescribed safety measure in schools. Safety drills are typically designed with the intent of simplifying and focusing people's responses in cases of emergency. Prescribed rules bring a group of children together, secure in the safety of adult-enforced limits. These are the rules. We will practice them. Follow them!

DIVERGENT THINKING

Divergent thinking complicates. It invites brainstorming: What are all the possible ways of doing anything, of solving any problem? Brainstorming offers a different sort of learning, asking children to share the responsibility for solving problems that affect us all. It addresses their fears directly, going beyond basic trust and obedience to ask for imagination and reasoning.

In Pasadena Sue Bush asked her 5- and 6-year-olds, "Does anyone know anything about earthquakes?" She scribed their words and read them back to the class. Then three smaller groups of children, each with an adult to help, met for discussion of all their suggestions. "Is that a good idea? Is that a good idea? Let's make two lists—one of good ideas, one of not-so-good ideas."

Children drew pictures and dictated stories, after the discussion. And then they all practiced earthquake drill in the different parts of their space, in the classroom and outdoors too. It went on all morning. One child, fearful that he wouldn't remember everything he was supposed to do, was smiling by the end of the morning, reassured by all that practice. It was clearly important to his teacher that *every* child learn this skill.

Since that day, more questions have come up. "What if the ground is shaking too much?" "What if you're in the bathroom doing a poop?" Children know what the really important problems are!

CHOICES FOR ACTION

Let's suppose you are a teacher and, as sometimes happens to teachers, there's a child who's driving you to distraction at group time. What could you do with him?

The convergent-thinking response may take the form of a behavior-management program. Such programs offer very specific plans to a teacher faced with an acting-out child. Typically they focus on the behavior, not on the child's possible reasons for behaving that way. Often they are logical-sequential, with prescribed consequences for first, second, and later offenses. The teacher follows the rules in her effort to get the child to follow the rules. If it works, it's the easiest way to go: someone else has done the thinking for you.

Divergent thinking, to be effective in problem solving, needs more practice than convergent thinking. It needs collaboration, too; you can't do it nearly as well all by yourself. But it can begin in your own head, at moments of frustration when logic and realism aren't required. Strong feelings and playful flights of fancy can go into the mix. In imagination, one doesn't have to be a responsible grownup all the time.

One teacher and her friend next door brainstormed these solutions within 5 minutes:

> Refer him to special education
> Give him more choices
> Don't give him any choices
> Put him in time-out
> Let him play with something he really likes during group time
> Take him on my lap during the meeting
> Lock him in the closet
> Ask him why group time is so hard for him
> Send home a letter to his parents
> Use my magic wand to make him disappear
> If he regularly pushes your buttons, try a preemptive strike. Go out
> of your way to pay attention to him before he starts acting up.
> Give him a hug first thing in the morning . . .

When brainstorming is used as a group problem-solving strategy, the next stage is typically, OK, let's sort out the possibles from the impossibles. And in a small group of thoughtful colleagues, several genuinely creative possibles may be generated, appropriate for trying with this particular child. Not a formula, but responsive thinking.

Behavior problems aren't the only challenges teachers face. The invention of scripted, "teacher-proof curricula" in literacy or mathematics is another example of efforts to build teaching and learning through convergent thinking by designated experts. Scripted programs tell a teacher exactly what to do in both teaching and guidance. They can be a great relief to new teachers, tired teachers, and teachers with other priorities in their lives. Someone else has done their thinking for them.

One of several problems with scripted curricula, however, is that everyone is supposed to take them seriously. They were written by experts, the district has paid a great deal of money for them, and they promise to raise test scores, to standardize children so they're all above average. But doing what's prescribed all day leaves no room for play, and there are many unscriptable, unpredictable moments at which learning-through-play will be the most effective possible way to teach.

> *Why did the dinosaur cross the road?*
> *Because chickens hadn't been invented yet.*

CHOICES FOR CONSTRUCTING UNDERSTANDING

Spelling as Play

Scripted curriculum is typically phonics based; that proves it's no-nonsense. But if there was ever a nonsensical proposition, it's English phonics—a useful tool only as long as you don't take it too seriously. All the rules of English spelling include *sometimes*. *Sometimes e* at the end makes the vowel say its name. *Sometimes* the long *a* sound is spelled as in *gate*. And sometimes it's spelled *rein, rain, freight, mane,* or *play*—and there are more. So we'd better keep playing with it!

To regard spelling as a tricky game may be the only way to survive it with one's self-esteem intact. Those with photographic memories for the shape of words are home free, but anyone who thinks phonics ensures accuracy in reading or writing English is in for disillusionment.

There are only a few ways to misspell Spanish, where most words come from Latin and most letters and letter combinations have only one sound and the exceptions are easily learned. (*"Be" de vaca o "be" de burro?*) There are only a few ways to misspell Japanese or Hawaiian. But English! with its roots in Old English, German, French, and Latin and borrowings from everywhere. And French! which is full of silent letters in its written form (and thus the daily *dictée* requirement for all French children). Some imaginative teachers of both these languages have invented an approach to spelling that begins with brainstorming rather than memorization. How many ways can you think of to spell the sound *nite*? Good for you! All those spellings work. But the ones that ended up in the dictionary are *night* and *knight*. How's that for crazy?

Play with words, their spellings and meanings and patterns, is of course a way that some adults amuse themselves all their lives.

Did you know that the finny creature that swims in the sea can be spelled *ghoti*? *F* as in rou*gh*, *I* as in w*o*men, *SH* as mo*ti*on. (Which rhymes with ocean, of course.)

Wordplay over the life cycle begins with infant babbling and moves swiftly into rhymes and tongue twisters and puns—and spelling and Trivial Pursuit and Scrabble. Probably the best memory aid for words, lasting lifelong, is to rhyme them and set them to music. Search your memory for your childhood and adolescent song/dance games; it won't take long to unearth them, verses and verses of them.

> *Wanna piece of pie?*
> *Pie too sweet.*
> *Wanna piece of meat?*
> *Meat too salt.*
> *Wanna drive a car?*
> *Car too full.*
> *Wanna buy a bull?*
> *Bull too black.*
> *I want my money back!*

That's from the hand-jives we sang and danced to as kids in my (Renatta's) neighborhood. I found out that my friend Beth, reared in a Black college town in Texas, grew up singing and playing the same rhyme. How quickly it came back to both of us, and how shocked were the other adults in the room when we got into it! The rhyme is still in my head, as are the songs we sang in the car when we were driving across the country to visit Grandma—"Comin' Round the Mountain" was our favorite, for the line "She'll have to sleep with Grandma when she comes." And the other day I was visiting a child-care classroom where the teachers were planning to introduce the song "Bought Me a Cat" to the children; they were trying to remember what each animal says and were not sure about the cat. I confidently assured them that the cat goes fiddle-I-fee.

With today's constant supply of DVDs and media entertainment to keep them mesmerized without effort, even in the car, how do kids learn to invent their own play strategies for coping with boredom? That's a basic skill they'll need all their lives.

How does anyone remember the alphabet? Because of the alphabet song, of course.

A teacher who finds this idea amusing is well prepared to teach spelling to 7-year-olds:

How do you write down the *aw* sound? Try *ought, brought, naughty, awful, call, haul,* and *shawl,* and then argue whether that's the same sound as in *morning* and *sawyer* and *sore* and *George*—keeping in your grownup mind that whether it's the same may depend on whether your pronunciation comes from Maine or Mississippi, Cornwall or Oxford, Edinburgh or Sydney or Singapore.

How did the egg cross the road?
It scrambled.

What do you call a chicken that crosses the road,
        rolls in the dirt and crosses the road again?
A dirty double crosser.

EVEN MATH CAN BE DIVERGENT

Math? That's where everything is right or wrong.

When math is taught with right-answer problems, winners and losers are guaranteed. But skilled teachers committed to leaving no child behind offer divergent learning modes—multiple-choice problems in which *all the choices are right.* It's the child's responsibility to choose which questions to answer and which answers to give—a more complicated challenge than relying on the teacher to make all the choices.

Suzanne's second graders play Money of the Day, with "coins" to manipulate on a flannel board. It's a popular game in her class, in part because money is something real, and just about everyone masters it (just as most people in this country, regardless of their grades in school, pass the written drivers' test and master driving cars at high speeds on busy roads. Driving is a demanding skill but a highly valued one).

During Money of the Day, Alberto and Mariana know all the answers, and Rosalva, who is still struggling with reading, mostly doesn't. But there's more variation than who knows/who doesn't. Cris, for example, has never volunteered an answer. Suzanne knows he understands the game, but Cris is one of those "slow-to-approach" children who watch and listen for a long time, until they have it perfect, before they speak up in public. This pattern is very common among second-language learners in a classroom or on a playground. A new language requires a lot of absorption. Some young children do the same with their first language, too, making a sudden leap from silence to complete sentences.

Suzanne asks, "How could you make $1.49?" It's a hard one; "How could you make $1.50?" would be much easier. But Cris suddenly raises his hand. He solves the problem in the most efficient way: 5 quarters, 2 dimes, 4 pennies. His teacher comments on that, and Cris twinkles at her (of course, he implies, this was *easy*). Can anyone think of another way to do it? Someone comes up with 10 dimes, 9 nickels, 4 pennies; someone else, with 149 pennies! Good thinking, all—and useful real-world knowledge when you find yourself at the checkout counter with no dollar bills but lots of change.

It's January, and Lucy is the only child who hasn't volunteered yet. She will. Rosalva, the struggler, actually did volunteer yesterday, for $1.00, and said, "Four quarters," with confidence. She's getting it, at her own pace.

A written review follows, and the question takes a different form: "Can you use seven coins to make $1.00?" Confident Cris is suddenly confused. (Learning proceeds in zigs and zags.) What if you began with quarters? suggests his teacher. "Twenty-five, 50," he begins uncertainly. "Oh yeah, that's half. Dimes—one, two, three, four, five. Seven coins!" Later he confides, "I was thinking they all had to be the same coin."

Where do New York kids go to learn multiplication?
Times Square.

And then there's multiplication, and the hurdle of the times tables. Memorizing is one thing, getting-it is another. As any primary teacher knows, children don't recognize what multiplication is *for* until they have personally discovered its usefulness as a shortcut. And that requires manipulatives: real things to count. Betty remembers asking her daughter's third-grade teacher, "Is there something she can count in the classroom?" And the teacher said, "You can look in the cupboard." It yielded only paper clips, but those are better than nothing. Renatta remembers working with her son in second and third grade, using manipulatives to reinforce his math learning. He became increasingly resistant, finally telling her that only little kids use things like that. That's for babies, even if it makes the tasks easier.

The need to count every item can continue for a long time for some children, surrounded though they may be by friends for whom the greater efficiency of counting by twos or fives is a no-brainer. To teach both groups of children at the same time requires games that are interesting as well as educational.

Thus, when some of his first graders didn't *really* believe that toes could be counted accurately by fives (the provocative question was, How many toes are in this room?), Mike Roberts said, "OK, off with your shoes and socks," and shed his too. The doubters had the task of counting every toe, one by one, until they were convinced that the answer was the same as counting feet by fives or persons by tens. And every child had a story to take home: "Know what *we* did at school today? We all took off our shoes and socks (and boy did they stink!)."

Shall we go on to fingers? How many fingers *and* toes are in this room? How many digits? (And that's a word with two meanings, related to the history of counting. Many words have two or more meanings. How come?) Good teaching includes many tangents, ideas to be played with, to sharpen the mind and create lasting enjoyment of learning.

> *When there are a dozen sharks and a fish, what time is it?*
> *Twelve after one.*
>
> *Why do sharks live in salt water?*
> *Because pepper makes them sneeze.*

I (Betty) told this one to my daughter, and she remembered one time when her little girlfriend threw her mom's best salt shaker into the neighbors' yard because their dog was barking. His name was Pepper.

3

Choosing One's
Play and Work

Assumption: It is more efficient to build action on
intrinsic motivation (what people want to do)
than on rewards and punishments.

What is the difference between a fish and a piano?
You can't tuna fish.

What washes up on really small beaches?
Microwaves.

Uncle Mo brought out his sketchpad and quickly, deftly, drew the dolphins leaping in the air. He said, "They remind you of being a child, with all that curiosity and energy. They remind you that this is what you could be, not what you should grow out of." (Creech, 2000, p. 153)

WHEN my (Betty's) son Don (who is now a wildlife biologist) was about 15, he and I went to Marineland on a cold wet November day. There was hardly anyone there except the animals—a wonderful gift for us. As we paused at the dolphin tank, we both noticed a volleyball at the edge of the pool. No one was in sight. Don looked at me, I looked at him, and he reached over the wall, picked up the ball, and tossed it into the pool. The dolphin bounced to the surface, grabbed the ball and tossed it back. My teenager was quietly ecstatic. Having no fish, he couldn't reward this behavior, so he simply tossed the ball back. The dolphin returned it. For 45 minutes they played catch. No fish were needed. Dolphins like to play catch. So do boys, even if they get soaked because dolphins don't care if they splash you.

Trainers at marine or zoo shows sometimes explain to their audience that they're not teaching animals new tricks. The respectful training of intelligent mammals, and of birds, too, relies on their natural behaviors such as leaping, swimming, or imitating sounds. We're not asking them to be something other than what they are. What is trained is the willingness to respond *on cue.*

Children can be trained in the same way, and often are. Behavior-modification plans set specific goals for a child and reinforce the desired behavior when it appears. Reinforcements typically serve as *extrinsic* motivators, and "throw him a fish" is a strategy used not only with dolphins and sea lions but also with little boys and girls who like goldfish crackers. At very early levels of development, food is the reward of choice.

But what's really to be desired is behavior for its own sake—like playing catch because it's a pleasurable, challenging game. That's why the dolphin was such an exciting companion; it chose to be Don's playful friend. The trick is to build teaching and learning on *intrinsically* motivated behaviors—what the learner *wants* to do.

WHAT SHALL I DO TODAY?

"The world is so full of a number of things," wrote poet Robert Louis Stevenson, and babies and toddlers are out to explore them all.

She has a rubber toy in her hand and is banging it up and down on the floor, giggling at the squeaks issuing forth. The toy bounces across the rug as she lets go, and she crawls happily after it. She stops to explore a string with a large bead on the end of it, then moves on after the rubber toy. She bounces it several more times before throwing it down, this time ignoring it as it bounces away. She returns to the string. She ignores the interesting bead on the end, but glances to see where the other end is. The string disappears into a pile of toys on the lowest shelf at the edge of the rug. She expectantly pulls the string and laughs delightedly. Then she catches sight of a bright red ball that has rolled out from the pile of toys that fell off the shelf. She crawls over to it and begins to smack it with her hand, making noises while doing so. She seems to expect the ball to move. When it doesn't, she tries again with more force. The ball moves slightly, and she moves after it. She is getting more and more excited, and as she approaches the ball, one hand accidentally swipes it so that it rolls some distance and disappears under a couch in the corner of the room. She watches it roll, starts after it, but stops when it disappears. Looking puzzled, she crawls over to the edge of the couch, but does not lift up the ruffle at the bottom to check underneath. She looks a little disappointed, but then she crawls back to the rug and the squeaky rubber toy. . . . She is once again banging the toy against the floor and laughing at the noise it makes. (Gonzalez-Mena & Eyer, 1989, p. 112)

And this is only part of a long observation. Baby watchers have endless patience, just as babies do.

The exploratory behavior of infants and toddlers is a fundamental example of intrinsic motivation. They are full of "satiable curiosity," but at this age they don't "ask ever so many questions" (Kipling, 1902/1978). They simply *do*. The young human animal has enormous energy for learning. Toddlers aren't afflicted by short attention spans; they are simply paying attention to *everything*, in their "world so new and all."

An observant adult who pays attention to every detail from the child's perspective, as in the above observation, shares in the joy. How can we help children sustain this joy all their lives?

Both imaginative play and skill learning are spontaneously initiated by young children who have the time and space to do so. Think, for example, about how many skills are involved in learning to tie one's shoes: Fine-motor skills, the ability to conceptualize in the abstract what the bow is supposed to look like when it is finished, and the bodily–kinesthetic skill to create in the real world what you know it should look like in your mind's eye. Renatta remembers:

I was starting school on Monday and I had my new saddle shoes. I could not tie them, and so my mother or my sister had to do it for me. I decided that I had to know how to tie my shoes! I could not imagine having to ask my teacher to help me with this, so I took my shoe and sat in the middle of my parents' bed until I figured out how to do it. I wasn't playing, I was problem solving, but somewhere along the line I had gotten the idea that I could teach myself to do this, and I was determined, so I sat there and worked on it. Surely my mother was aware that I was in the middle of her bedspread with my shoes, but she left me alone. I suspect she told my sister and my brother to leave me alone too.

I learned to tie my shoes that afternoon, and in doing so knew I was ready to go to school. Almost 45 years later I remember how good I felt when I could tie my shoe each time. That feeling of confidence and mastery is something I draw on whenever I have something new to learn. I don't always go back to learning to tie my shoes, but I do know that I can learn what I need to learn when I need to learn it. I cannot tell you how valuable this has proved to be in my life. Maybe I would have figured it out in a Velcro world, but I would never want to chance it.

We could argue in favor of getting rid of Velcro shoes, digital watches, and pull-ups, for the sake of children's learning to tie shoes, tell time, and toilet themselves. Children, however, are ingenious in finding alternative opportunities for learning. When I asked my college students to write about something they learned through play, one wrote about playing police officer and tying up her friends. "That's how I learned to tie," she explained.

What did the mama rope say to the baby rope?
Don't be knotty.

Young children are self-propelled to achieve as well as to explore. It's important to recognize achievement not only in academic terms, but also in such concrete areas as tying one's shoes, making friends, and exercising the muscles of the imagination.

WHAT SHALL WE DO TOGETHER?

Angela, age 3, arrives in the house play area, picks up a doll, and says: "Baby, you need your bottle."
    Cesar, who has been driving a truck around the room, now brings it to the stove, cooks "soup" in it, and feeds it to the teacher sitting nearby. Then he carefully wraps up a doll and hands it to the teacher: "Here's your baby, OK? I'm covering your baby up, OK?"
    He spreads a cover on the floor for himself. So does Angela, saying: "I want to go to sleep."
    Vivian, who has joined them, promptly becomes the mama: "I'm gonna whup you. Get under there with your sister."
    The two children lie down together and Mama covers them. Angela pretends to cry: "I want my bottle."

Vivian: I'm gonna feed you with the spoon.
Angela: Can I have some more 'ghetti?
Cesar: Mama, look at my toy.
Vivian: I bought you that for Christmas.
Cesar (covering himself again): Mama! Mama! Mama!
Vivian: Go to sleep.
Cesar (as Angela takes his cover): My cover! My cover!

Mama Vivian tries to cover him, but Angela takes that cover too. However, Angela relents when he lies down in the baby bed, and she covers him there.

Cesar (out of bed and wandering around): Mama mama mama!
Mama: Lay down!

The sociodramatic play of 3- and 4-year-olds enables them to talk and act out familiar experiences, propose play ideas, and jockey for leadership.

This isn't yet sophisticated group play, but it actively involves several young children in spontaneous child-directed activity, as they practice the care and feeding of babies, cooking, and getting other kids to play with them. All of these are lifelong skills; learning how the world works begins here.

A bonus for adults is that young children at play are usually too busy to be bad. This teacher is free to sit and observe—and even be fed! "You can eliminate behavior problems if what you are asking children to do is engaging for them. When they're engaged, they don't want to throw something across the room—they need it" (LaFlamme, n.d., p. 31).

By the time experienced players are 5, some of them can organize a group of friends almost as well as an adult can.

Several of the kindergarten children decided to move and rebuild the obstacle course, which is constructed of large "loose parts," including tires and a balance beam, and is a very popular activity during outdoor time. This challenging task was initiated by Olivia and planned and carried out with no adult assistance. "Ready? One, two, three, lift." "Whoa, put it down for a second. Someone's gonna get hurt." "OK, right over here."

Matt, Clarence, and Trisha are inventing tossing games with the bean bags. Toss them into the buckets: "Here, two for you and two for you." Take turns collecting the tossed bags and being the tossers. Try a bigger challenge: Toss them into the tires from the top of the climber. "Wait a second; don't throw yet. You might hit her. Let her have a chance to move out of your way."

PLAY, WORK, GAMES, AND LABOR

In these stories, the younger children were spontaneously exploring (the baby) and interacting in sociodramatic play (the 3-year-olds). The 5-year-olds were initiating individual (shoe tying) and cooperative work—activities with a plan and a purpose. These busy children are accomplishing the developmental tasks of early childhood: trust, autonomy, and initiative (Erikson, 1950). They are choosing what to do. Children *want* to try new things, get good at skills, create patterns, make friends, and make decisions. All these behaviors are supported by the availability of materials, time, and adult awareness of what's needed when.

No point in starting anything there. They never let you finish.
Don't get interested. You'll just get interrupted.

These are school lessons I (Betty) once heard out loud from my 8-year-old and also observed in his little sister's kindergarten. They describe children's experience in classrooms segmented into short arbitrary time bytes. While learning to accept interruption is a necessary part of the socialization process, it also limits intellectual development. So it is useful to look at the balance, in any educational setting, between intrinsic and extrinsic motivation as experienced by the different members of the group (including the teacher).

To support the next developmental task, *industry*, in the primary-school years without losing the strengths fostered in preschool, teachers must find a balance between *play, work,* and *games*, all of which can be intrinsically motivated. *Labor,* the fourth option we discuss here, requires extrinsic motivation—threats or bribes. Here are our definitions:

- *Play* is open-ended. The individual is free to explore a wide range of possibilities, with no pre-established rules of procedure or outcomes. Being competent in play means being self-directed, able to find something to do, to get absorbed in it, to discover things in the process and go on to more elaborated play or to self-defined work.
- *Work* is undertaken to achieve a significant product—a building, a painting, a clean room, a tasty meal. It is real work only when the product is experienced *by the worker* as significant—that is, as demonstrating his competence in ways important to him.
- *Games* involve testing one's competence within the limits of a pre-established structure. A game requires conformity to a set of rules, an understanding of the underlying consensus. The individual who is good at games is able to follow the rules and to win a reasonable proportion of the time. Games are there to be won.
- *Labor* is a response to a pre-established structure, but it lacks the sense of optimism and challenge and joyful completion experienced in a good game. It may be socially useful in some context but, unlike work, it yields no significant product. Because it doesn't get the worker anywhere, external rewards or punishments are typically necessary to keep her at it. The learning which accompanies labor is extraneous, having to do with the acquisition of skills for survival in a setting lacking personal meaning.

(Jones & Prescott, 1984, pp. 85–86)

The paper-and-pencil tasks that dominate the day in many classrooms may be experienced by a child either as games (meaningful tests of competence) or labor (tasks that you have to do but that don't make personal sense). Such tasks don't produce anything real; there's not much you can do with a completed worksheet except toss it in the circular file in the corner. They're games for the children for whom they're well timed—the winners—unless they're too easy to be worth doing. For the losers, they're mostly frustrating, and discipline problems are a predictable outcome. For a child who doesn't get it, forced labor, fooling around, and daydreams are just about all she has to do in school.

Making everyone do the same thing guarantees both boredom and failure. There's no way to design a closed task that fits everyone. If it's boring for children, it's often boring for teachers too. It is, however, possible to design skill-practice activities with many right answers, transforming them into lively games. (See spelling and math stories in Chapters 2, 6, and 9.)

Skill practice is needed. So are play and work—opportunities to choose, interact with peers, and create useful products individually and collaboratively. Practicing skills that are already developed, children draw pictures, tell and write stories, construct objects useful and beautiful. Projects may be assigned, with scheduled time to work on them. In small groups, children may read a book together and decide how to share it with the class. Individuals may create a display of what they know about a favorite animal or plant or place. Classrooms focused on such activity are noisier and more interesting than those where everyone sits and works quietly all the time. More learning happens in them.

And they're messier, more like programs for younger children where a lot is going on. Children do drop things as they move on to the next activity. (When we were arboreal primates, we were free to throw our banana peels on the forest floor for some smaller critter to pick up and devour.) Cleanup is almost nobody's idea of fun—and so we're back to labor and extrinsic motivation and dire consequences.

> *Mom: Go pick up your room.*
> *Kid: I can't. It's too heavy!*

> *What did the broom say when it got tired?*
> *"I'm feeling sweepy!"*

Unless ingenious teachers can make it interesting.

TRANSFORMING LABOR INTO GAMES OR WORK

In a school-age child care program that included a long outdoor play/work time, some of the kids had gotten into fort building. If you're seven or eight years old, forts are serious business; you need lots of scrap lumber and real tools. Gina, the teacher, agreed with this premise, and she provided both.

But at the end of the afternoon, at clean-up time, she was often furious: "Andre, you were using the hammer! Where is it? Go find it now!" And Andre would shrug his shoulders; he's not building now, he's tired and hungry. It's the teacher's problem, not his.

So Gina called a class meeting and made it everybody's problem. "There will be no tools today because people aren't taking care of them." (Protests from the fort-builders: "But we need . . .") "I know you need them. Your forts are great. But tools are expensive and you have to be responsible for them. What can we do?"

After brainstorming with the kids, fort-building time that day was replaced by a massive organized search for tools—with great success. Then Gina went home to think. And at the next day's class meeting she introduced a complicated check-out system, with a daily clipboard list for each set of tools, a space for each user to write his or her name, and the admonition, on pain of dire consequences, that every tool had to be checked back in before going indoors for singing time. With an organized plan, Gina got to be appropriately ferocious (which the kids enjoyed), they got to learn some responsibility skills and practice name-writing, and the forts continued to thrive.

Tim (age 8): All the teachers this year are terrible.
Gina: You're right. We're ogres.
Tim: All the teachers last year were ogres, too.
Gina: That's what we're here for. You should be proud to know you're
    being taught by some of the best ogres in the country.

                                                        (Carney, 1978, p. 60)

When there's a task like cleanup to be done and nobody finds it intrinsically motivating, one response is to organize games with rules. The sign-in chart was an interesting puzzle, the drama of dealing with ogres was highly satisfying, and the winners got to use real grownup tools in their self-chosen work.

Another response is to make it a choice for those children ready for real work that uses skills they've practiced in their play. In second grade Suzanne has, of course, organized cleanup tasks for everyone. These are often experienced as sheer labor, except on those days when the class responds to the game of "Pick up everything off the floor in 3 minutes. Ready, set, go!" But her new challenge is the piles of children's work papers on her desk and in the corner on the floor, for which she was criticized by her supervisor yesterday. (Teachers are supposed to be tidy at all times.) She has just figured out a filing system, with labeled dividers organized by the different subject-area work times of the school day. That will help her find things when they're needed—but when will she, while supervising children through the day's transitions, find time to put the papers into the file box? It's time to brainstorm with us, her colleagues.

Remembering some good advice from a kindergarten teacher, "Never do anything for the children that they could do for themselves," we see the possibilities. "Do you have any kids who could file papers and would thrive with the responsibility?" we ask Suzanne. "Yes, Lupe and Sara—and Cris, if he didn't goof off," she says. "So could you organize the papers on your desk by subject area, and whenever you see one of those three kids with a free moment, say "Sara, can you put this stack of papers in front of the MATH tab in the file box, for me?"

If Sara is intrinsically motivated to help you by doing this real job, she'll welcome the opportunity and do it cheerfully and well. If she's ready to learn to file them alphabetically, even better. If she says, "But I need to finish reading this chapter," you can say, "Fine, go ahead," and then try Cris. This is helping-as-privilege, and it requires no reward except a Thank you. It's what teacher's pets have always gotten to do, but the collection of odd-task helpers can expand from week to week as some other kid complains, "How come she gets to do that and I don't?" To which the answer is, "But you do. Lupe, will you show Alberto where the math papers go, so he'll know next time I ask him?"

There's skill learning built into this plan, as well as buy-in as a member of a responsible classroom community. This strategy acknowledges the usefulness of Vygotsky's (1978) concept of the *zone of proximal development*— the area of competence in which children need a more experienced co-player to see the activity through. "We're all helpers here" can be simply syrupy, hopeful teacher-talk, or a genuine description of a class in which children are increasingly self-motivated to make it work, because it's so personally rewarding for them. Those children who aren't ready to file papers can be put off unless they really want to try; and maybe motivation will see them through.

Inviting children to play, giving them choices, is a way of complicating what goes on in a classroom. Play, by its open-ended, unpredictable nature, complicates. Many teachers, especially inexperienced teachers and those under administrative pressure to keep order and cover a prescribed curriculum, are searching for ways to simplify. For that, they need to become effective dictators. Authoritarian governance simplifies: It prescribes the rules and enforces them. Effective rules create not smarts but obedience. (Behind the scenes, of course, they create rebellious play—and the persecution of other, weaker kids, following the authoritarian model.)

Smart teachers engage kids in play and games, and smart kids define important work for themselves. Intrinsic motivation liberates. The revolutionary leaders of the American colonies, fed up with an authoritarian monarchy, and declaring their independence, asserted these truths to be self-evident: "that men are endowed by their Creator with certain inalien-able rights—and among these are life, liberty, and the pursuit of happiness."

They were, from our perspective, opting for a society based on intrin-sic motivation: pursuing happiness for the individual while respecting the rights of others to do the same. Over the centuries we have broadened this definition of democracy to include, in principle, everyone. Is that possible?

What did the vacuum say to the broom?
I wish people would stop pushing us around.

4

The Democratic Vision

Assumption: **Democracy is a better bet than dictatorship. Sharing power is safer than trying to hang on to it all. To liberate is wiser, in the long run, than to domesticate.**

What do sea monsters like to eat?
Fish-and-ships.

How do you know the ocean is friendly?
It waves.

Why won't clams lend you money?
Because they are shellfish.

SAFER doesn't mean easier. If you have enough power, as boss of the world or of your classroom, it's easiest just to tell everybody else what to do. In the short run, dictatorship, overt or subtle, is more efficient than the long drawn-out process of genuinely democratic decision making. And once you have power, you're likely to be reluctant to share it. But power is easily abused.

The abuse of power incites those who don't have it to (a) think up ways to get what they want/need without being caught, or to (b) plan revolution in the name of social justice. Every American schoolchild is taught that armed rebellion in a just cause is a noble enterprise; that's how the land of the free and the home of the brave, our democratic society, began. The hard part came next, and it's still going on. Responsible citizenship in a democracy is a challenge requiring lots of practice. Where better to practice it than in school?

Relatively few schools, however, offer children real practice in democratic decision making. Children en masse are a threat to grownups: their potential for creating chaos is high. Most schools are designed for the domestication of children.[1] "Children can't be given freedom," as one principal said, "until they've learned responsibility" (by which he meant obedience).

What happens if a teacher looks into a bright light?
Her pupils shrink.

Like many other teachers, I (Renatta) remember my student-teaching experience with a supervising teacher who told me not to smile until October. You can be nice to the children once they're intimidated. The principal in this school had adopted the role of tyrant, as many principals do, serving as an ever present model for teacher behavior as well.

While my supervisors were much more experienced than I, they were less accepting of the liveliness of young children. Two days before winter break and 4 days before Christmas, I was attempting to do a lesson with a group of squirmy, excited first graders. Their wiggling and fidgeting were unbearable. I asked all the children to stand up, and I raised my hand. I told them that when I dropped my hand I wanted them to scream as loud as they could. When I raised my hand again they would have to stop. I did, they did, and then we completed the reading lesson. Satisfied expressions on the faces of the children replaced the fidgeting, and the remainder of the morning was uneventful. Once I had joined their game, giving it an interesting shape, they were willing to join mine—the lesson.

"What was going on in room 2 this morning?" sniffed one teacher in the lounge during lunchtime. "I let the children yell," was my unexpected response. Nothing more was said in my presence.

If children are to grow up to be responsible adult citizens, their school curriculum should focus strongly on *playing at being a citizen*—a community member who practices sharing responsibility for solving the community's problems.

You know this has been achieved in a class of older children who don't explode when the teacher leaves the classroom. They go right on doing their work, not because they fear punishment for misbehavior, but because they have bought into the importance of maintaining a collaborative community. Children as young as 4 can buy into responsible problem solving and can practice strategies for doing so with one another. They learn democracy most effectively through play. Play and democracy are noisier, messier, and more time-consuming than conformity to authority.

The 4- and 5-year-olds in a classroom whose teacher is committed to teaching democracy were losing control toward the end of a busy morning. So she brought them together in the whole group with a new idea for the game of Musical Chairs, modified to avoid leaving anyone out of the game (a penalty too great for children this young to bear). "Walk around the circle while the music is playing," she explained the rules to them, "and each time I'll take a chair away. When the music stops, find yourself a chair; and if someone can't find a chair, invite them to sit on your lap." In this classroom, we take care of our friends. "Hey Charlie, squeeze in next to me," called Bill. It's math, it's language, it's following rules, and it's fun!

What kind of gymnastics do you do in January?
Wintersaults.

DEMOCRACY (LIKE PLAY) IS ABOUT . . .

... making choices
... negotiating choices
... sharing decision making

With these skills, continually honed for the rest of one's life, one can thrive as a responsible member of a democratic community. The process of making choices that include choosing potential friends begins in very early childhood. To keep a friend, it's necessary to master negotiation and sharing—and that's basic curriculum in the preschool years. In infancy and toddlerhood, the predemocratic curriculum is focused on choosing and doing.

Making Choices

As a baby becomes aware of the world, she starts distinguishing its contents (toes, Mommy's nose, a rattle, the fuzz on the blanket), tries them out, and learns to play with them. Each month she becomes more selective, and by the time babies are a year old each displays distinct preferences in selecting what to do when the basic needs for food, sleep, and comfort have been met.

Here's Harry, a solid, alert child of 10 months who displayed no interest at all in walking:

Harry and his very social mother would enter the play group eagerly greeting other parents and children. At some point Harry would be placed in a square toddler chair, which offered him proper support and an unobstructed view of what was going on. He would play with whatever material was on the table and scan the room until he caught someone's gaze. That someone—parent, teacher, or mobile child—would make his or her way over to Harry. "Hi Harry Barry!" was a common greeting. Whatever the greeting, Harry would laugh!

He had a wonderful deep chuckle, laughing with his entire body. The children liked to hear him laugh, and so they gathered around him, made eye contact, and did things to make him laugh. He became the center of a hub of activity by sitting there, looking from child to child, and laughing.

Harry had it all figured out—no need to walk, let the world come to him. It did, every time. It was another 5 months before Harry walked, when he was good and ready.

Toddlers in group care spend a lot of time just checking out the territory: What's to do here? Running around is, of course, one of the most interesting things to do, practicing mobility skills. Poking other toddlers is another fascinating thing to do. It is also appropriate, since each toddler lives in his own world, where everything and everyone exists for his exploration.

Choice making begins as an individual activity, with "Me want." In a group, it gets complicated by the presence of all those other makers of choices—planets revolving within a very small system. When two or more toddlers are in the same space, "Mine!" rears its insistent head. Toddlers are not at all democratic. They want what they want, and it's mine. If I want it, it's mine! If I ever had it, it's mine! If I have one at home, it's mine! *Conflict resolution* and *conflict maintenance* become constant curriculum in groups of 1- and 2-year-olds, as adults guide children's learning of these important skills. Through socialization, we teach toddlers to be less honest about what they want and more careful of others. Care for others is essential to democratic living.

In a democratic classroom for children of any age, children make choices. For substantial parts of the day (which may be called play time, work time, preferred-activity time, choice time, English-language-development time—whatever the teacher and children prefer or can get away with), the lesson to be learned is, Use your time wisely and well. Choose to do something you are really interested in; ignore the other interesting choices, for now. Share space and ideas with others, be respectful, and check them out for good ideas. Plan, engage yourself, and continue until you're done. (No one unpracticed in these skills can get through an American supermarket without a seriously overburdened credit card. Say yes, say no. And don't waste time dithering.)

It takes practice to become a skillful chooser. Good preschools provide that practice as a matter of course. A preschool teacher who moved into second grade was surprised to find that her 7-year-olds, unlike her 4-year-olds, had had little previous practice in making choices from among learning-center activities for math and science. The resultant confusion led her to resort to the strategy common in kindergarten/ primary classes: rotating children between centers in assigned groups.

She'd like to teach them more independence, but things get noisier if choice is permitted, and her principal strongly disapproves of both movement and noise at school.

Who gave tickets to dinosaurs?
Triceracops.

Negotiating Choices

In a democratic classroom, children receive consistent adult guidance in conflict resolution and social problem solving. Adults don't arbitrarily use their authority to resolve children's disputes ("If you can't play nicely, then we'll just put it away," "He had it first. I'll set the timer and after 5 minutes it will be your turn.") Instead, whenever possible, problem solving is given the time and adult attention it deserves, because of its importance in the early childhood curriculum. Further, *conflict maintenance* is a value.

Many people—women especially, teachers especially—see conflict as something to be avoided. Under what conditions can people (big and little) who differ with one another *sustain* their conflict, seeing it through to resolution rather than cutting it short? Most commonly, conflict is cut short through the exercise of power by the stronger individual or group; for example, a teacher puts a child in time-out. This silences the opposing voice and whatever wisdom it may carry.

The democratic ideal—never fully realized—is that all voices contribute to collective wisdom and all should have a turn to be heard. (Jones & Nimmo, 1999, p. 8)

Democracy begins in conversation.
—John Dewey

Four- and 5-year-old children who have had the opportunity to observe adults mediating disputes and other problems may spontaneously *play at being a mediator.* Marina's teacher told us, when we asked her for examples:

The other day Jasmine wanted the rope swing and Patrice wanted the rope swing. Marina was watching interestedly, so I asked her if she had any ideas. "You could play a game where you could both use it," she told her friends.

Diego was yelling because Alan was digging near his hole, and Alan was yelling back, and Jacob said to Alan, "Why don't you have your hole right here? That way his dirt won't get into your hole."

What could be simpler? If you've heard these words often from your teachers, and you're watching your friends having this dumb argument, you can figure it out. You can even help them figure out what to do when they're sad, if you've seen teachers doing that.

Samantha is new to the school this year, and she was crying very hard because her mother had just left. Old-timers Marina and Ysabel were there to offer comfort. "I miss my daddy," said Ysabel. "I'm going to write him a letter." "I'm going to write my mommy," said Marina. And when this strategy didn't stop Samantha's crying, they got some different paper and started drawing and cutting out hearts—progressively smaller ones, creating heart families—and showered Samantha with them until she couldn't keep crying any more.

And this is truly practical literacy. How can you tell your friend and your family that you love them? By using your writing and drawing skills; that's what you've been learning them for.

Sharing Decision Making

By the time children are in preschool, having learned the basics (Don't bite. Use your words.), they are ready for group guidance in problem solving and decision making. They are also embarking seriously on the challenge of making friends: Will you play with me? To be a friend, one must learn to take turns and give in graciously, as well to assert one's own fascinating ideas.

A schedule that includes extended time for sociodramatic play guarantees that children will engage frequently in shared decision making within their minidemocracy. Who's got the power? Can I win, or do I have to give in this time? Or can we invent a win/win? Laurie Read (1993) tells this story:

I enjoy watching kids role-play adult issues and come up with their own creative solutions. One day Mark and Joanna, a boy and girl who are 4 year old best friends/enemies, were in the doll house mutually caring for a doll. The play changed when Mark suddenly got up and announced, "G'bye, honey, I'm going to go to work and be a fireman now." "But you can't go," Joanna piped up. "I have an important meeting today and you have to care for the baby." (I was in hysterics.) They got into a mild conflict, Mark (shaken) maintaining that his job was to go to work, while Joanna persisted in saying this was an important meeting and she had to go to work. "Besides," she firmly stated, "I got my briefcase to the door first so I have to go."

I kind of hovered nearby, waiting for the bloodshed, but they went into a wonderful negotiation about whose job was more important. (Interestingly, both parties felt it was a given that each had an important job; this was a conflict about *today*.) Ultimately they decided they *couldn't* resolve this issue, so they came to a wonderful compromise. They went and got a younger child, Sarah, out of the block area and made her the baby sitter! The best part was that she actually stayed, rocked and fed the baby. Mark and Joanna went off to work. About 20 minutes later they came back and paid her with a suitcase full of Monopoly money. (If only we could all be paid $100,000 for 20 minutes!)

It was a classic, hysterically funny thing to watch. I did go to them separately later and congratulate them on dealing really well with a tough problem. (pp. 83–84)

Disagreements are aired, roles and scripts are negotiated, rules of the game are argued, because children *want* to play together and thus have remarkable energy, ingenuity, and patience in making democratic decisions in which everybody wins and therefore won't go 'way mad. Strategies may run the gamut from intimidation through majority rule to genuine consensus, as children mature in empathy as well as in reasoning. They use their words a great deal, and language is developing apace. Children practice language skills more effectively in interaction with peers than in structured group language lessons from a talkative adult.

As children master group play skills, the teacher's role is increasingly that of observer. But she keeps her responsibility for the leadership of large-group conversations, through the early childhood years. As the structural rules for such meetings are learned, children increasingly take responsibility for sharing leadership. The goal, in all this skill practice, is effective membership in a democratic community in which all voices are heard.

Observing in a prekindergarten program strongly influenced by Dewey, Kerstin Moore (1998) wrote:

Many aspects of daily life in this classroom came about through group discussions and decisions. As an example, it was the practice in this classroom to read a story as a group at the very end of the day. The teachers noticed that because the children were often so busily engrossed in their activities it was hard to interrupt them for a story. Why not do away with the story? So the teachers decided to put the question to the group. They introduced a voting box, and each day everyone would have the opportunity to cast their written vote into the box.

Voting for reading a story or not became an important aspect of the daily routine in the classroom. Children assumed the responsibility for counting the votes and tallying the results, teachers shared some of their decision-making power. Important issues came up for discussion: Does everyone only get one vote? Should teachers get to vote? Do only boys vote for no stories?

A couple of boys objected to teachers voting because they assumed that all girls vote yes for a story and there is only one boy teacher. Besides the gender issue, the children raised a lot of other interesting ideas for the teachers that we talked about amongst ourselves before bringing it up with the children again: Did the children care whether the voting was or was not anonymous? How do the children perceive the teachers, their power, and their alliances? How are teachers a part of the group? Should they be part of group decisions? (pp. 45–46)

Discussions like this can go on practically forever, as anyone knows who has tried them. They aren't a recipe for decisive action; for that, a teacher in charge is what's needed. They are, rather, "the kinds of real-world experiences with which Dewey meant to engage children's minds" (Moore, 1998, p. 63). They are democracy as *curriculum*, emerging out of real problems as they happen. Where teachers are able to build on day-to-day reality, no canned human-relations curriculum is needed.

More problems surface in democratic classrooms than in authoritarian classrooms. Thus there are many more opportunities to practice listening to other points of view, asserting oneself, and learning to respect both self and others as people with rights and voices. Learning to live together in community, day in/day out, is basic curriculum. (Jones, Evans, & Rencken, 2001, p. 105)

> *What did Cinderella wear to the beach?*
> *Glass flippers.*

> Mother: *Did you take a shower?*
> Billy: *I didn't know one was missing.*

BUT IT'S HARD!

By hanging on to power we are trying—as teachers or parents or managers—to maintain stability, to keep to the vision by which we live, to make sure things don't get broken. These are good and noble reasons. They are practical, too; children are not yet ready for responsibility and need control.

Power is, however, easily abused. The abuse of power is nearly always rationalized by the powerful as having virtue and as being necessary, at least in the modern world, which has been infiltrated by democratic values. In eras in which absolute monarchy was accepted as right and proper, the arbitrary use of power didn't have to be justified to the masses; it was the divine right of kings armed with the sword and the guillotine (and of schoolmasters armed with the hickory stick). Some monarchs were recognized as virtuous, some as evil. Power, it has been said, corrupts; and absolute power may corrupt absolutely. The same risk hangs over teachers, in charge of very little people.

Children often resist what adults want them to do. Dogged resistance and even full-blown tantrums, in the child under 2 or 3, are useful practice in *wanting*. Wanting is basic to making choices. Democratic governance is based on electoral choice. Nobody makes good choices without practice.

Since small children have very little real power, their wanting should be acknowledged rather than shamed, in order to support the self-esteem and pride necessary to mental health. You really want your mommy to stay, don't you? You're really sad. You're really mad, too. The boundaries should be firmly set; children aren't in charge of the world. But they are vulnerable and deserve all the nurturing we can give them, so they may retain a hopeful view of life—the basic sense of optimism that enables them to do their best.

For those who are in charge, moral autonomy *and* mental health are required for acceptance of the necessary checks and balances on power. It is easy to exploit children. And if democracy is difficult to achieve even among consenting adults, it is still harder to create a democratic classroom (and nearly impossible in a nondemocratic school). The teacher/leader in such a space must constantly balance have-to's with the sense of humor that enables her to take the point of view of the child (though she will undoubtedly have lapses toward the end of a long hard day). She needs problem-solving strategies that include the children rather than stopping them short.

Democracy is the worst form of government except for all those others that have been tried.

—Winston Churchill

AND DIVERSITY MAKES IT HARDER

Democracy is hard to achieve. It requires flexibility, willingness to play fair, and attentiveness to the expectations and wants of others. It's even harder in a multicultural society, where language, values, and assumptions about how life should be lived on a daily basis can't be taken for granted. Dewey believed that it's the diversity of thinking available to a democracy—where, ideally, everyone's voice is heard—that makes it smarter.

Potentially, diversity enriches democracy. Practically, it is often exasperating.

"Why, why don't these parents teach their children English before they come to school?" wailed the principal of a school in an immigrant neighborhood to an English-speaking parent in an unguarded, unthinking moment. "They'd be so much more successful then."

The temptation, for members of the majority, to look down on those *others* becomes part of the social fabric, even where the official creed is that all of us are created equal. ("But some are more equal than others," George Orwell pointed out.)

"Democracy is built on reciprocity among strong egos," wrote John Dewey. Perhaps many invented social categories—race, caste, and class among them—simply reflect the tendency of strong egos to resist reciprocity and to regress to the "Mine!" of the passionate toddler, in the fear that there might not be enough to go around.

NOTE

1. Brazilian educator Paulo Freire (1970) asserts that education either domesticates or it liberates. Learners can be tamed to obedience or freed to take initiative on their own and others' behalf.

5

Bicultural Competence

Assumption: **Becoming consciously bicultural is more powerful than either assimilating or maintaining separateness.**

What do you call a cool rabbit?
A hip-hopper.

How do rivers stay cool?
They go with the flow.

Why is it always cool in a sports stadium?
Because there's a fan in every seat.

CULTURE is a shared collection of symbolic forms and traditions. It includes all the rules for appropriate behavior, including language, learned through membership in a particular community. It brings its members together while separating them from other communities of people.

Being bicultural is the result of a dual socialization process. It requires the capacity to hold more than one idea in one's head at the same time and thus to be able to imagine and experiment with relationships between them. Piaget (1951) called this capacity *operational knowing* and said young children can't do it, at least not in a testing situation. But in their real lives, many children do.

I walk into the Head Start classroom and sit down on a child-sized chair, notebook and pen in hand. A 4-year-old girl glances my way with interest as she continues a conversation with her friend. I start to write about her play, and she keeps an eye on me as she stirs an imaginary mixture in the pot on the playhouse stove. *"Comemos pronto,"* she says to her friend. *"Tienes los tenedores?"*

"Es buena sopa, Nina?" the teacher calls to her from across the room. *"Yo puedo olerla. Huele muy deliciosa."*

39

Nina smiles happily. Then she turns to me. "What you writing?" she asks. "I'm writing about children playing," I tell her. "You writing about me?" she asks. I nod. "Show me where." I do. "What do it say?" "Nina speaks both Spanish and English," I tell her. Her grin is wide.

And I (Betty) envy this child's skills in code-switching. She has never seen me before, nor has she heard me speak. Yet she has correctly guessed from subtle visual cues that my first language is English, and she confidently uses it in initiating conversation with me. We share pleasure in her accomplishments.

Knowing two languages can make children smarter, write Cronin and Sosa Massó (2003).

Learning a second language as a young child [creates] "cognitive flexibility." For example, bilingual children can easily recognize that *pelota* and *ball* are merely words representing a round object used for playing games. . . . monolingual children have a harder time understanding that "ball" is a name arbitrarily assigned—as it is hard to explain to a young child that her sister is also my niece: "No she's not, she's my sister."

As pre-operational thinkers, young children can usually hold only one attribute in mind at a time. However, young bilingual children have the opportunity to understand language on a deeper, more abstract level . . . because by speaking two languages they automatically know that there can be two words for the same object. . . . All children at first perceive the name as part of the object and later realize that the object can have multiple names, but knowing two languages helps that shift to occur earlier and easier. (p. 81)

Although research based, this assertion has little influence on American educational policy. To a remarkable degree, American schools and the public attitudes that shape them are dominated by a *subtractive* view of bilingualism, a belief that a language other than English is a handicap in an English-dominant society (which has been populated by many immigrants, but the Brits got here first). Most schools emphasize neither maintenance of home language nor support of two-way bilingualism (in which English-speaking children are expected to learn a second language while nonnative speakers learn English).

To lose one's mother tongue in favor of another language is subtractive: it takes away one's identity. *Additive bilingualism* (Cummins, 1986), however, enriches. Each new language offers a different worldview that is never entirely translatable. Languages, like other aspects of culture, reflect all the ways of living in the world.

Around the world, bi- and multilingualism is the mark of an educated person—one who can reach out to life beyond the local community. The United States was settled by speakers of many languages, and in many areas it is multilingual today. But the language of power is English; by custom and by law, all children must learn English, and the unexamined American assumption that we're the best pervades our lives. Or at least the lives of those who grew up as part of mainstream American culture.

Luisa, age 7, is embarrassed when her teacher asks her to help a new, monolingual Spanish-speaking student in their class. "Does my teacher think I'm like that country girl?" she wonders. Bernie, her big brother, quickly looks away from the bus window at the sight of a brown-skinned man going through a trash can for recyclables. "Go back to TJ [Tijuana]," he mutters, ashamed that someone who looks like himself is doing something that others look down upon. Both these children of immigrants have learned about their own culture through the filter of the dominant culture and its attitudes toward outsiders. Are they fortunate enough to have confidently bicultural adults in their life, with whom they can discuss such awkward moments?

SAME IS NOT EQUAL

Although the civil rights movements of the past half century have created a rhetoric of "political correctness" that acknowledges past injustices based on race, culture, and gender, the pressures to assimilate, to give up one's origins as the price of access to the mainstream, are embedded in our social fabric. And so we find ourselves, in the name of equal opportunity, driven by a national effort to standardize education for all, no matter who they are.

Uniform curricula and standards imposed at district, state, and federal levels ignore the obvious fact that different children learn differently. Young children entering kindergartens that offer no opportunity for play quickly discover that there is one right answer for practically everything. Some kids—those from the cultural mainstream—already know those answers; others don't.

Not long ago I (Betty) visited a charter public school where all the children (the majority of them native English speakers) study Spanish daily. I began my observing in a second-and-third-grade classroom where Blanca, a native Spanish speaker, seemed inattentive most of the time. She joined group discussion only when called on, talked to her neighbor during seatwork, and didn't finish her page. She's a child a teacher might worry about. But when I followed the children as they moved on to Spanish class, I saw a different

Blanca; here, she was teacher's helper and star pupil. She spoke clearly and fluently, glowing with pleasure as she raised her hand at every question. It was her turn to play at being smart—which she is.

Can we do it?

Sí, se puede!

But some of the usually smart English speakers were having a hard time, a new experience for them. Some of them may go home and complain; some of their parents may complain on their behalf, if they're accustomed to being winners in the system. People with power are strongly invested in holding on to it—and handing it on to their children. Even those who give lip service to the vision of an egalitarian society expect *their* children to be more equal than others. Standardized testing in English-only serves such families well, since tests are designed to create winners and losers. The privileged are good at ensuring that it is their children who continue to win.

Groups experiencing oppression have to take action on their own behalf, since those who hold the power are disinclined to notice those who don't (Delpit, 1995). Biculturation strategies name and respect more than one way of being in the world, and teach them to the children.

Yolanda, a Black kindergarten teacher in a Black inner-city school, valued her children's home language, which she herself spoke at home. She also wanted them to learn school language. She identified a half-hour period daily in which "We are all going to practice talking the way folks talk at school." During that period she corrected the children's speech, and they corrected one another. *Paying attention to how we talk* was the curriculum for that half hour. For the rest of the day all speech forms were accepted as valid communication.

What did one firefly say to the other firefly?
"You glow girl!"

What do you call cheese that is not yours?
Nacho cheese!

To grow up smart and respectful of others in a diverse world, children—all children—need opportunities to show what they know and to discover what they don't know. They need time to play with children like them and not like them. Some need help in learning how to make friends. They need time and varied opportunities to learn new words and rules and ideas, individualized and not only regimented. They need their experience named and acknowledged by teachers. Their parents are entitled to know what happens at school and why and to be honored for the values by which they are raising their children. And their teachers need to be supported in making their own good judgments about how to teach these children in this time and place.

Regimentation of schools and teaching undermines the development of bicultural competence. Play, in a bicultural context, is crucial in preparing children from diverse backgrounds for competent learning.

PLAY TIME AS PART OF LANGUAGE LEARNING

Some years ago I (Betty) visited a New Mexico prekindergarten for English language learners. For the first half hour of the day the children were free to play. The room was alive with conversation. Then the resource teacher arrived for the ELD (English Language Development) lesson, and the children sat in a circle while he showed them drawings of faces and asked what feelings each face showed. He talked a lot. When children responded it was evident that many were simply guessing (just as young children do when asked the day of the week during calendar time). They didn't have much to say.

At the end of the lesson he noticed that I had been taking notes and he asked if I had any suggestions for him. He hadn't worked with such young children before, he explained, and could use some advice. "Do you really want me to tell you?" I asked. When he nodded, I explained that I saw him doing most of the talking. "If this is language development time, you're getting a lot more practice than they are," I said. "They were getting a lot more during play time."

Kathleen Evans, teaching a kindergarten class of Iu-Mien children from Southeast Asia, whose home language is oral, not written, was challenged to learn all she could about their culture while introducing them to English language and literacy.

I had a lot to learn about them, what they were interested in, and what they thought about. . . . I was confident that they would thrive in a classroom in which action, talking, and thinking were expected. . . . I built shared understandings best by watching them at play, then introducing activities that connected with what they already knew and did. (Jones, Evans, & Rencken, 2001, pp. 59–60)

To provide time for learning through play, Kathleen modified the official curriculum:

We had a mandated English Language Development time, one hour per day, and the administration's idea was something highly structured, systematic, and explicit. I felt that my English-language program was the net cast over every part of the day. I told the official from the bilingual office that he was welcome to spend a week in my classroom if he needed convincing.

And I knew, to the exact date, when each child had mastered a skill. (p. 128)

TWO-WAY BILINGUALISM: CULTURAL BRIDGE-BUILDING

In many Head Start and child-care centers in the Southwest, I (Renatta) have noticed, the English-speaking teacher communicates with the English-speaking children. The Spanish-speaking aide communicates with the Spanish-speaking children. There is rarely an attempt to support communication between groups. The only members of the class who are fully aware of everything that is going on are the bilingual children. Their confidence shines out.

One year I was determined to break this pattern in a Head Start class I visited weekly. My conversational Spanish is at preschool level, but I spoke to children in whatever language they were using. On the playground, I noticed, the adults rarely interacted with children; they watched and talked among themselves.

Instead of joining the adults, I followed the children. I tried to extend their play, for example, by bringing blocks into view to add to a construction project. If a new child approached, I helped him join the activity. If I didn't understand something said in Spanish, I would ask one of the bilingual children to interpret for me, thus allowing them to help other children and make connections across language differences. I soon noticed that wherever I was on the playground, there were all the children. They weren't riding bikes or climbing on the other structure, they were wherever I was.

It was tiring but satisfying. The other adults wondered why someone would come from a college to play with the children. What did I see in the children's play that was so important? a couple of them asked me.

I am fluent in two languages: Standard American English and Ebonics, the home speech of many African Americans. Standard English gives me an edge in academic and other public settings; Ebonics, with my own folks. I am not at all fluent in Spanish, and so the real Spanish speakers, even at age 4, have an edge when I'm trying to talk to them in their language. Everybody needs an edge some of the time, in order to develop confidence and use his or her power respectfully. Everybody needs to be the underdog from time to time, to learn how it feels and develop sensible strategies for dealing with that reality.

What has four legs and goes ticktock?
A watch dog.

What does a dog wear when he's swimming?
Doggles.

We will argue that, ideally, all young children should learn two or more languages, for these reasons:

- Children should become fluent in the dominant language of their society, in order to have full access to its expectations and opportunities.
- Those of recent immigrant origin should retain the language of their grandparents, in order to maintain caring relationships and family influence on their behavior and values and to have a home to go back to as needed.
- Those whose families speak only the dominant language will have more choice from among possible second languages. To be English-only is a handicap.
- Early childhood is indisputably the best time to acquire pronunciation and fluency in a second language. Language acquired before the age of 10 is typically unaccented.
- Literacy is most easily learned in one's first language, then transferred naturally into the second.
- Children should sharpen their thinking and their understanding of diversity by practicing code-switching at appropriate times and places.
- Bilingual adults have access to wider opportunities in employment and culture.

But what second language should be taught in a society in which immigrants speak dozens of different languages? In Los Angeles we daily hear and see Tagalog and Mandarin, Farsi and Armenian, and many others—but predominantly Spanish. While president of the National Association for the Education of Young Children, Lilian Katz (1993) made a case for Spanish bilingualism nationwide, because it's our largest second language and is spoken in most of our neighboring countries in the Americas. She wrote:

Of course, for many of our children, English is a second language, and Spanish would be a third. A bilingual nation is not an impossibility, as some other countries have shown. It is my impression that we underestimate children's language ability and many other intellectual capacities. (p. 2)

THE ROLE OF PLAY IN BRIDGING CULTURES
AND DEVELOPING SKILLS

Remember Alejandro? He's the little boy with three big sisters who hasn't yet learned to build with blocks at age 5. (See Chapter 1.) In his very academic kindergarten, block-building skills aren't on the list of standards, so they aren't taken seriously by the teacher. Blocks are available only occasionally, at the end of the day when the children have finished their work.

When there are only 20 minutes of play time, the smart builders aren't going to waste it by being nice to Alejandro and helping him learn what they know. They have an airport to get built in a hurry, so they shoo him out of the way before he knocks it down. When does Alejandro get to be competent in kindergarten? When does he get acquainted with the kids who might be his friends, speak his language, know how he plays, and play with him?

In academic kindergartens, it's only the children who come from homes with educational toys and parents who like playing school who discover, to their relief, that school is a familiar place. During hands-on literacy activities they get to play with manipulatives and talk to their friends, while Alejandro is one of the half dozen kids sent to the remedial teacher for more-of-the-same sit-still phonics. Not surprisingly, these kids space out or act out.

Alejandro's teacher thinks he can't do anything. Kathleen, who focuses on developing bicultural competence, learned what her Mien children can do by observing them at play (they're remarkably cooperative players) and creating a classroom to support spontaneous practice in their two languages and two cultures.

Ghosts and spirits, fishing, sewing, caring for babies, cooking, and constructions all emerged as curriculum areas to include that reflected the children's home culture. The office, bookstore, hospital, shampoo factory . . . all emerged prominently as aspects of learning to share in the culture of power. (Jones, Evans, & Rencken, 2001, p. 68)

First-grade literacy teaching is likely to ignore even more completely the skills and interests some children bring from their home and community experiences, while making strict demands for sitting still and keeping quiet. In contrast, Anne Haas Dyson (2003) tells vivid stories of classrooms where the principle of "friends learning to write" lets children talk as they construct stories and spelling together.

Noah: What you like to eat? What you like to eat? Pizza? Uh, candy canes? Um—
Wenona: Candy canes! . . . I'll write "candy canes." How you write it?

Noah: Um C, C-A. (saying word to himself) No no no. Yeah. A-N-D.
    That's all.
Wenona: That's [CAND] "candy cane"? That's not right.
Noah: Yes it is.

(p. 109)

In first grade children aren't very good at writing yet. They communicate with one another through talk and drawing and play. Using these established skills, they can support one another as they work to master this new one.

INTERPRETING PLAY TO PARENTS AND OTHERS

But if it doesn't look like school—if children are talking to one another, inventing stories, lying on the floor as they write—a principal may regard the class as out of control. A parent who knows what real school looks like may wonder, Aren't they teaching you anything in that school? Why are they letting you play? School is where you practice obedience, respect, and the work ethic. It is not for playing around.

I (Renatta) sent my son Alex to an African-American independent school in first grade, and I loved its cultural emphasis. Other parents applauded when the director explained, at an assembly, "Our 4-year-olds do not have time to play. They have plenty of class work, and homework every night." Parents were reassured that an educator, Black like them, understood the pressures that the children will have to face and was teaching them early about hard work and achievement. I, with a developmental background, felt that rote-memory tasks are meaningless to children who lack the concrete hands-on experience that supports real learning. Alex stayed there for only a year.

When play is viewed as "messing around," it's hard to see its importance in the curriculum. It's also a leap of faith to trust a teacher who tells you that play is important but who can't demonstrate to you why or how it will benefit your child in the future. If you want parents to trust you as an educator, you'd better be able to demonstrate the importance of play in a convincing manner. (Cooper, 1996, p. 94)

This requires strong curriculum building and planning, designing play environments that support learning, and then explaining to parents how they work. Many parents will accept a play-based program with more confidence if some of the trappings of school are present, even in classrooms for four and five year olds. A writing center which offers spontaneous practice with school tools—paper, pens and pencils, crayons and markers, scissors and staplers—can include letter and number stencils, *key word* cards, blank books to create stories in, note pads, and clipboards, and an attentive adult ready to listen to children's stories and write them down. Manipulatives with built-in shapes and colors, puzzles, even simple worksheets that can be used to *play school* without having to meet too-demanding expectations for accuracy— these things look like school. Books, too, are familiar parts of school, and children to whom adults read often will also *read* to each other playfully, practicing page turning, left-to-right sequencing, and story memory as they do so. (Cooper, 1999, pp. 56)

IT'S SMARTER TO BE BICULTURAL

A multicultural, bicultural-competence perspective implies that a more consciously diverse society—one in which everyone, not only recent immigrants, is challenged to learn some of the ways of the other—is desirable. Why might this be so?

It's safer. If I share city streets with you and have no understanding of how you talk and think, we are strangers and therefore at risk with each other. Once upon a time in the American South, Black folks walking on the sidewalk were expected to step into the gutter if a White person approached. It was too dangerous for both to be on the same sidewalk. Tribal thinking—Us and Them—leads to fear and hostility and bloodshed. Gang warfare wasn't invented on the streets of L.A.; it has a long history.

My (Betty's) father, born before the turn of the century, White though not English-speaking at school entry, became increasingly anxious in his old age as Oakland's Black population increased; he didn't know these folks. His grandchildren, with two generations' advantage in hanging out with lots of different people, are much more relaxed than he. His 6-foot grandson casually commented to me about racial differences, when in his teens: "If I feel like getting into a pickup basketball game, I can decide where to go. If I want the kids to be shorter than me, I go down to Glassell Park. If I want them to be taller than me, I go to Northwest Pasadena."

It's more interesting. As the strange becomes familiar and the familiar strange, all of us have access to one another's exotic music, food, and visual culture. Shall we order pizza or go out for Chinese? is among the many taken-for-granted choices in any American city. The world's cultural discoveries provide rich play opportunities for us all.

For a confident teacher, a class of children from unfamiliar backgrounds is a new learning challenge. "Teacher research" is sophisticated play. It's what experienced teachers do to stay lively and curious, as well as to become increasingly effective in their work.

It's more productive, because it includes everyone. There's strength in coalition. Bernice Johnson Reagon (1983), a veteran of civil rights and women's movements, asserts:

There is no hiding place. There is nowhere you can go and only be with people who are like you. It's over. Give it up.

At a certain stage [she explains] nationalism is crucial to a people if you are going to ever impact as a group in your own interest. Nationalism at another point becomes reactionary because it is totally inadequate for surviving in the world with many peoples. . . .

It must become necessary for all of us to feel that this is our world. And watch that "our"—make it as big as you can. The "our" must include everybody you have to include in order for you to survive. I ain't gonna live unless you let me live. Now there's danger in that, but there's also the possibility that we can both live—if you can stand it. (pp. 357–359, 365)

Biculturalism invites play and social problem solving through divergent thinking. It is, therefore, a way to help all children get smarter. The hardest challenge lies in teacher education and staff development. Can adults unaccustomed to but often actively discouraged from "acting smart" on the job, in their work with children, be supported to do so? Can a school become a trusting environment where intelligent risk-taking by both adults and children can be practiced? Will you be my friend? Can we play together?

POSTSCRIPT: LANGUAGE LEARNING AS PLAY

Children learn a second language not by listening to translations or drills; they learn by interacting with others using understandable, easy language that they hear others speak. . . . If the input is challenging and they can figure out the meaning, it engages them and they learn. That is why play works so well as a vehicle of language acquisition: children learn new structures by understanding messages that contain new structures. Play also offers a child many opportunities to hear language in various contexts and to figure out what the playmate is saying. (Cronin & Sosa Massó, 2003, p. 97)

El Lobo

Jugaremos en el bosque, mientras el lobo no está. Porque si el lobo aparece a todos nos comerá.

   Lobo, estás ahí?

   ¡Sí! Y me estoy poniendo la camiseta.
   ¡Sí! Y me estoy poniendo los pantalones.
   ¡Sí! Y me estoy poniendo la camisa.
   ¡Sí! Y me estoy poniendo el sombrero.
   ¡Sí! Y me estoy poniendo los zapatos.
   ¡Sí! Y me estoy limpiando la casa.
   ¡Sí! Y vamos a jugar—Tu lo traes!

                        (pp. 100–101)

If you are a Spanish speaker, you have an advantage at this moment. The other jokes in this book have been in English, giving others the advantage they've learned to expect. But this funny situation comes from another language and culture. If you've ever played this song-game, growing up in a Latino community, your personal memories may make it even funnier. It's your turn to be smart, because you're bilingual and have the power of code-switching.

If you're not a Spanish speaker, what did you do just now when you encountered *El Lobo*? Did you skip over it, since it clearly wasn't in your language and you're not used to that disadvantage? Did you pause long enough to try to figure it out? Probably most Americans understand *sombrero*, and perhaps *casa*. Do you enjoy playing with words? (If you do, notice how you go about it and what's fun about it. It's a skill all children should learn. Don't peek at the translation below;[1] that's only for the monolinguals who haven't the energy to play right now.)

If you're playing in the woods and the wolf is lurking in her house, getting dressed and sweeping the floor and then COMING TO GET YOU! you'd better pay attention even if you don't know the language. In this game, the group of children walk around the edge of a circle while the wolf, in the center, pretends to put on items of clothing, one by one. "Once the wolf is 'fully dressed,' she chases the children until one is caught; the captured child becomes the new wolf. Every time the children walking on the circle's edge call out to see if the wolf is there, they do not know whether the wolf will put on yet another item of clothing or will chase them. The child playing the wolf may prolong the suspense by naming every possible item that can be worn" (Cronin & Sosa Massó, 2003, p. 100).

Teaching second-language learners, children or adults, Sharon Cronin provides real clothing, with labels in Spanish. A Spanish-speaking wolf begins the game, then remains in the circle to mentor the next wolf, who can simply put on the clothing while the mentor says the words. Listening precedes production, in language learning. And action makes it memorable.

NOTE

1. *El Lobo* is a Latin-American song game described by Cronin & Sosa Massó (2003, pp. 100–101):

We're playing in the wood, while the wolf isn't here.
Because if the wolf appears, he will eat us all.
Wolf, are you here?

Yes! And I am putting on my T-shirt, pants, shirt, hat, shoes. And I am cleaning the house. And we are going to play—you're it!

6

Letting Children in on the Secrets

Assumption: **Giving things their right name is a better idea than keeping names secret.**

DAUGHTER: *Why is my brother acting like a chicken?*
MOM: *Because he thinks he's a chicken.*
DAUGHTER: *Why don't you tell him he's not?*
MOM: *Because we need the eggs.*

DOG TO CAT: *It's a dog tradition. Every morning and evening, we thank God that we're not cats.*

NAMING gives power. *Representing* an experience, in words or pictures, saves it to think and talk about. Stories and images are ways to organize events for oneself and, through sharing them, to invite the construction of collective meaning.

Pain, put into words, can be transformed into strength through psychotherapy. Oppression, talked about in meeting after meeting, can be transformed into nonviolent (or violent) revolution. Delight can be re-created in a pastoral symphony; terror, in the painting of a scream. The nameless fears of childhood can be confronted in a picture book, where the Wild Things are tamed by a brave child. Respite from real-life troubles can be found on the fantasy island of a storybook and, perhaps, enable serious imagining of other lives for oneself, to be realized in the future.

Play with names and images is the basis of all art and science: What have we here? How could we rearrange it—for fun, for beauty, for practical problem solving? Scrabble, the gardens of Versailles, and the Golden Gate Bridge all began in play.

WHAT'S THE PASSWORD?

Daddy: "Want to be in the club? What's the password?"

Kathy, age 4, shouting triumphantly: "Great-grey-green-greasy-Limpopo-River-all-set-about-with-fever-trees!"

The reward is a shared hug and a lifelong love of Kipling's Just-So story "The Elephant's Child" (the password's source), read by father to daughter many many times.

Names are passwords into the secret world of grownups. Grownups know everything. Kids don't know anything, for starters, but they begin learning as soon as they're born. Before the end of their 1st year they have begun to learn language, the names of things. Words are powerful *place-holders*; they enable human beings to hold and re-create experiences in the mind, in order to think about them and to talk with others about them.

As soon as children can talk, they start being excluded from grownup secrets. Little pitchers have big ears, and so secrets are whispered or spoken in the grandparents' language. In African-American culture children may be allowed to stay in the room during an adult conversation, but only if they lie low. "Keep out of grown folks' business," is the harsh rebuke to the child or adolescent who dares to speak up, and being sent from the room follows.

Literacy gives still more power. Historically, in authoritarian societies it was often denied to large segments of the population: slaves, peasants, women. The right to knowledge has been reserved for the few. The ideal of universal literacy goes hand in hand with the ideal of democracy—which needs an informed citizenry to work.

The democratic ideal is freedom—freedom of speech and the press, freedom of information and knowledge. There are set boundaries, but the preferred risk is usually too much knowledge rather than too little. Add modern technology, including television and the Internet, and the risks of information overload ("The news never stops," our local news radio station reiterates) and of telling children too much become abundantly clear.

However imperfectly, democracy gambles on the faith that knowledge is safer than ignorance. Applying that idea to the education of young children replaces a "don't ask, don't tell" mentality with an "ask and tell" process that invites children's naming and thinking at an early age.

There's a lot of precedent among preschool teachers, and even babies' educarers, for naming children's experience out loud, in respectful ways, and encouraging them to do it for themselves. *Use your words* is among our most familiar mantras.

Which words? What needs naming for children? Here we're proposing strategies for naming (a) power, (b) adult behaviors, (c) feelings, (d) arbitrary rules, and (e) possible solutions to problems of all sorts.

NAMING POWER

Few cultures invite children to question authority—to ask and then think through, with adult support, their guesses about how the system works. Whatever is, is right. That view makes sense in an authoritarian society, in which respect is a one-way street.

I (Renatta) remember a talk I once gave to a group of family child-care providers, in which I spoke of treating children with respect. A provider who was very popular with parents in the neighborhood looked at me with disdain. "Children are supposed to respect adults," she grumbled to those sitting near her. "Why does it have to be one or the other? Couldn't it be both?" I asked. But I realized that our different views probably reflected how respected we felt in our work worlds—I as a college professor, she regarded as a baby sitter. Power is one of the things polite people don't talk about.

We are not saying that children don't need authority. For health, safety, and general sanity, adult power over children is a necessity. Children's questions, however, can be addressed on two counts: (a) naming the reasons for rules and orders, and (b) frankly acknowledging the existence of power inequities (and thereby providing children with a direct invitation to reenact this drama in their play, as they take turns at Big Mama, The Cops Are After Us, and All the Teachers Are Ogres).

Problems arise if parents and preschool teachers, having bought into the reasons for giving children reasons, lose track of the boundaries between words and behaviors. Children deserve the privilege of naming, but not of misbehaving. When I (Betty) was a preschool teacher observing other adults getting sucked into endless arguments with children, I wrote in exasperation one day:

A child who always wins in verbal conflicts has scant foundation for confidence that adults, most of the time, know what they are doing. . . . Children are often asking not "Why do I have to?" but "Do I have to?" So it is that a simple affirmation of the way things are—"Because it's time to go home"— is ordinarily a more appropriate response to the question, "Why do I have to go home now?" than something along the line of "Because it's time to go home because it's lunch time and all the children are going home and the teachers are going home and so you can come back tomorrow . . ."

A young teacher was explaining at considerable length to a child the reasons why he must not do what he had just been doing. Finally, not certain he had been listening or had understood, she asked, "Now Pablo, what did I say?" He replied calmly, "You said, No." (Jones, 1961, p. 8)

Pablo is good at naming, and accepting, power. His teacher can learn something from him about when to use her words and when to shut up and move on. Sometimes the appropriate response to "Why do we have to?" is simply, "Because I said so, and I'm bigger and meaner than you." When Pablo's grandpa says, "Move your rusty butt NOW," Pablo moves. He knows not to argue with Grandpa when he's not in the mood. Wait and catch him when he's mellow. Grownups' feelings are powerful; respect them.

In their homes and families, kids who use their smarts to scope out other people often figure these things out for themselves. In early childhood programs, however, we take conscious responsibility for *teaching* skills and knowledge that we believe to be important. In this context the important things, including power, should be named. They're part of the curriculum.

NAMING ADULT BEHAVIORS

Even babies can learn from adults who use their words in this way. Naming behaviors and talking to infants are at the core of Magda Gerber's work in Resources for Infant Educarers (RIE)(Gerber & Johnson, 1998). Take advantage of each caregiving interaction—diapering, feeding, bathing, those things that happen every day all day—to involve the child as an active participant in the process. Tell her, "I'm going to get you a clean diaper," and let her hold it while you clean and powder her bottom. Respect her by telling her what you are doing now and are going to do next, and respond to her visual and physical responses. Don't distract her with a mobile or a rattle; don't talk to other people instead, as if the baby isn't a social being too.

When a child is respected by being let in on what the grownup is doing or planning, he is often more inclined to cooperate. Take, for example, the 5-minute warning common in early childhood programs: "In 5 minutes it will be time for cleanup . . ." Children absorbed in self-selected activities are entitled to know if they're going to be interrupted. This is both respectful and practical as a guidance tool; children who have been warned may be somewhat less resistant when the final deadline arrives. If they were listening to the announcement, the words have offered some processing time in their heads. Words make planning ahead possible.

It often happens that teachers from other cultural backgrounds fail to provide the clarity that many African-American children have come to expect from adults. I (Renatta) was once asked to observe Vernon, a 4-year-old whose teachers couldn't get him to come inside for group time.

"Do you chase him?" I asked. "Oh no," they assured me, but it was easy to see that they did. Clearly, he enjoyed the game.

The group went in and I stayed outside with him. "Who are you?" he challenged me.

"I'm gonna help you get inside today. Are you ready to go in?"

"No!" he assured me. His mama should have put him on a track team, the way he got down into sprint stance.

"I'm not gonna chase you."

He knew better. "Yes, you are."

"No, I'm not gonna chase you." This dialogue continued for several rounds until he asked, with much less assurance, "You're really not gonna chase me?"

"Nope. I can't run as fast as you. I'd look pretty silly if I chased you. I'm not here to chase you. I'm here to help you get inside."

He put his hand in mine and we went inside.

NAMING FEELINGS

Molly Scudder (1978), an exceptionally straight talking teacher in her conversations with children, has written:

The areas of human experience which evoke the strongest feelings are those which I call *the tender topics*. . . . Some of these topics—appropriate ways of expressing feelings, embarrassment, school difficulties—come up all the time in the classroom. . . . *Accepting strong feelings as part of the curriculum* makes for a different sort of school. The teacher steps down from the pedestal and out of the authoritarian role, since if children are people with feelings, so is she. (pp. 37, 36)

Because I (Renatta) had studied child development before my son was born, I had learned this attitude. But it doesn't match my cultural experience, and while I often talked respectfully with Alex, I also yelled at him sometimes. He, however, attended the same preschool in which Molly taught, and so at age 4 he said to me, "You're not spozed to talk to kids that way." I knew where he had learned that. Alex is now grown up, and he still says to me, "You don't have to raise your voice," when I yell.

Developmentally appropriate early childhood programs are the places where feelings are most likely to be planfully named for children. Use your words. Tell him how you feel. Tell me what you want. I may tell you, "You can't have that wish, my Little Bear" (Minarik, 1957), but you know I know, and that's important. And I love you. Good teachers of toddlers name feelings for them all the time. Children are good at learning those words. Yelling "I MAD!" and stamping your foot is a better idea than biting; it gets your feelings out and your message across with less damage all round.

> *Do not meddle in the affairs of dragons.*
> *For you are crunchy and taste good with ketchup.*

Respectful teachers name their own feelings too—sometimes out loud and on the spot. Containing a screaming toddler is stressful for teacher, child, and most likely for any watching adults as well. Saying clearly and calmly "I'm holding you now, to keep you safe. When you're ready to keep yourself safe again, then I can let you go" reassures both the teacher involved and any observers that she does know what she's doing, that her behavior is planful, not punitive. Professionals are people who know and can explain what they're doing, who can make their expertise transparent. (The fairly recent trend, in some medical settings, to talk patients through procedures rather than just doing unexplained things to their bodies has been very reassuring to this sometime patient! [Betty])

As children get a little older, good preschool teachers name other people's feelings as well. "You hurt her feelings when you wouldn't let her play with you. What can we do about that . . . ?" And they can even introduce literacy as a tool for communicating one's own strong feelings:

Richard . . . is sad about his mother's departure and has been crying for some minutes. The teacher invites him to join [the children who are involved in a writing activity]. "Here's some yellow paper. Write Mommy a note and tell her you miss her." Pointing to the container, she asks, "Would you like to choose a pen?" Then, "We'll give Mommy the note when she comes to pick you up this afternoon."

Literacy gives power. Richard stops crying immediately, though he continues to look sad. He clutches the pen high above the point, making letters and letter-like forms. The teacher sits close to him. (Jones & Reynolds, 1992, p. 64)

In a responsive classroom, we study things *because they happen*. No lesson plan can predict the emergence of serendipitous opportunities for learning.

The eruptions of feelings that happen unexpectedly in the best of classrooms can be deplored, ignored, or selectively transformed into curriculum. Feelings that are ignored generally reemerge in some mutation that disrupts learning. Living together in restricted space, day-to-day, is even more challenging than the three Rs. (Jones, Evans, & Rencken, 2001, p. 155)

NAMING ARBITRARY RULES: SPELLING

At school, you will remember, we are supposed to spell all our words right. Teachers and dictionaries know how to spell. Children do not, and writing time is punctuated with cries of "Teacher, how do you spell . . . ?" But children with beginning familiarity with the sounds that letters represent can competently invent their own spelling—nonstandard but often readable even by adults. "GNYS at work" wrote Paul on his do-not-bother-me-I-am-busy sign, and his mother didn't even correct his spelling when she used it as the title of her book about Paul as writer and reader (Bissex, 1980).

But at school we spell correctly. Of course, but that should be the end point of an editing process. First get the words down on paper; don't worry about anything but the story you want to tell. When it's time to send a letter home to parents, or when you want to bind your story for the class library, then we'll edit it to be sure it's written right. That makes it easier for other people to read. Nobody but you can write your story, but all writers need editors.

"But teacher, *night* is a dumb spelling! It ought to be *nite*. The silent e makes the *i* say its name—see, I remembered what you told us."

"Good for you, Juanito, you did remember the rule. But the people who write dictionaries and the people who make tests have decided to break the rule and spell it *night*. They're bigger and meaner than we are. If you want to write 'This is the moon at nite' on your drawing, I can read that just fine. In our class, you can choose. But when we're doing a spelling test, then we're going to follow the big people's rules. It's important to learn those too. Just the way you've learned to read English and Spanish, too."

People *made up* spelling. They talked before they wrote. "We can make up spelling too," the teacher tells the children. "You do it every day. I'm a pretty good reader of new spellings, but sometimes I have to ask you, don't I, to read me what you wrote because I don't get it? Just as sometimes you don't get words you're trying to read."

As we pointed out in Chapter 2, spelling is one of many problems that can be approached by divergent thinking. So can arithmetic, and other people's feelings, and even safety drills.

NAMING POSSIBLE SOLUTIONS
TO PROBLEMS OF ALL SORTS

What could you do if there's an earthquake?
What are all the ways you could spell *night*?
She's crying. Can you think of some ways to make her feel better?
How many ways can you tell us "eleven?"

Literacy and numeracy can be introduced as (a) facts to be memorized, (b) games with rules, (c) opportunities for playful invention.

Anne's first graders really like the game of *"How many ways can you tell
us eleven?"* (or three, or sixty-four, or one hundred and twenty-two . . .).
They play it nearly every day, with variations. She keeps making it harder,
now that they're veterans at it. It's as playful for her as it is for them; she
gets to keep thinking what ideas to bring up and which to just let go,
for now.

Anne: How many ways can you tell us "eleven?" I've just told you one way.
I've said a word out loud: e-lev-en. Does anyone know how to write that
down?
      Yes, Jannie does. ELEVEN. She used letters from the alphabet.
      "I know!" yells Julio. "Write a 1—and another 1!"
      Anne: Like this? (writing them 2 feet apart)
      Julio: No, silly! Right next to each other.
      (Anne fixes it. You used numerals, she remarks.)
      Monica has another idea: Write ones while I count. One, two, three,
four, five . . .
      (Anne is writing 1   2   3   4   5.)
      No, not like that! You didn't listen to me. I said "Write ones."
      (Anne apologizes, erases her numerals, and writes 1   1   1   1   1
1   1   1   1   1.)
      Anne: Is that eleven?
      Children: Count them! Use the pointer. And don't go too fast.
      Anne: OK. Count with me . . . (They do, and it's right.) Monica, I have
a question. How did you get just the right number and not too many?
      Monica: I just counted up to eleven and then I stopped.
      Anne: But that confused me, because you were saying 2, 3 and you
wanted me to keep writing 1, 1. Is there another way we could do it? If
you had said 1 eleven times, could you have kept track of how many?
      "You could count on your fingers!" bursts out Shandra.
      Anne: Good idea. Let's all try it. Do you have eleven fingers? (Predict-
ably, they run out at 10.) What could you use now?
      "Your nose! Your big toe!"

Anne (who has been thinking about asking next, "Is 1   2   3   4 etc. another way of writing 11?" or quick-drawing a row of 11 little ducks, but decides to go in another direction instead): OK, let's just practice using numerals now. We've written 11. How else could you write eleven? Do you remember what this means?   10 + 1!   5 + 5 + 1! 2 + 3 + 4 + 3!   (Count those fingers again, says Anne.)   + 2! (Got it! says Anne.)   12 – 1!   (Hey, you thought of a new way to go!)

Eligio's hand is waving frantically. "I thought of another different way to say eleven. *Once!*

(Anne is bilingual enough to get that one.) Yes indeed, the word in English is eleven, and the word in Spanish is *once*. You write it like this: on-ce. ONCE.

(Teacher play-in-her-head time again: Shall I point out to these 6- and 7-year-olds that in English *once* is a totally different word and it's pronounced *wuntz*, not *ohnsay*? Nope, let that one go, unless a child brings it up. Let's try a different question, and then stop; the wiggles are beginning.)

Anne: How do you write ONCE in numerals? Right, 11. How do you write ELEVEN in numerals? 11 again. Amazing. Do you think maybe math is bilingual?

"All this nonsense just confuses the children!" complains an impatient, frustrated observer of this lesson. "Just teach them how to do it and be done with it. This messing around is a waste of time, and it doesn't teach them that math is serious."

That's true (but few of them were confused. They had their thinking caps on). Instead, it teaches them that math, like all other classification systems human beings rely on, was invented by people, and we are inventors too. We can *think*. We can think *together*, because we don't all have the same ideas, and so we keep learning new ideas from one another.

What kind of refund do you get at a football game?
A quarter back.

Adults can model problem solving as play, to enable children to learn to do it too. Playing with possibilities, using words, is language development, practice in critical thinking, practice in social skills—listening, taking turns. It's very basic curriculum, offering skill practice in using language in real-life situations, with others. These skills are important both for further academic learning in school and as a wonderful lifelong mode of recreation for those who are good at them.

NAMING AS PLAY (AND ALL THE OTHER ARTS)

A panda walks into a café. He orders a sandwich, eats it, then draws a gun and fires two shots in the air.

"Why?" asks the confused waiter, as the panda makes toward the exit. The panda produces a badly punctuated wildlife manual and tosses it over his shoulder.

"I'm a panda," he says, at the door. "Look it up."

The waiter turns to the relevant entry and, sure enough, finds an explanation.

"*Panda*. Large black-and-white bear-like mammal, native to China. Eats, shoots and leaves." (Truss, 2003, quote from book cover)

Get it?

When you're a kid, life is full of things you don't "get." Jokes, puns, double entendres, the point of the story/end of the movie. I (Betty) had to go see *The Sting* a second time, as an adult, because the denouement was so fast and complicated that I got lost in what had actually happened. I just went to see the third Harry Potter movie (*The Prisoner of Azkaban*), and even though I had read the book, I wasn't quite sure at the end who the good guys and bad guys had turned out to be. I had to ask my grandson to explain it to me. Adults can help explain to kids, kids explain to one another (you're not cool unless you get it), and sometimes it's the kids who get it first. We're naming for one another. It's usually funnier if you got it the first time, whatever it is; but there's a whole series of layers of "getting it" as one gets older. That's even true of *Winnie the Pooh*; for some 5-year-olds, it's very serious stuff. *Alice in Wonderland* is a masterpiece of levels of understanding, to be enjoyed equally but differently by children and by adults. People derive some of their pleasure in in-jokes from being one of those who understand them. For example, the dog-to-cat joke (from a cartoon from the *New Yorker*) at the beginning of this chapter is mildly funny for those who like dogs, but really funny for those familiar with the traditional Jewish prayer in which men thank God that they are not women.

By naming things for learners, we deepen their understandings and enrich their memories. The arts name and envision experiences for all of us; they are provocations that sharpen our senses and insist that we pay attention to the shapes and meanings of things. The opportunity to experience and to create art is an essential part of learning for all children. The arts are not frills. Hands-on science is not a frill. Incessant focus on literacy and numeracy out of context, as drill, guarantees that they will remain meaningless in the life context of some children. The real evaluation question is not, How does this child score on a reading test? but, Will this child read for pleasure and for information once he has left school? In our short-sighted emphasis on testing all children and turning curriculum into test preparation (even in kindergarten), we have lost sight of the real purpose of schooling: to prepare children for the rest of their lives.

Where do cars swim?
In the carpool lane.

Why was the computer tired when it got home?
Because it had a hard drive.

LEARNING TO NAME OUR TEACHING PRACTICE

I (Renatta) recently read that the test scores provide 400 ways for schools to fail and only 1 way to succeed. But test scores (they're numbers, so they must be scientific) seem to reassure people that teaching is going on. There are other ways to document children's learning. Teachers under pressure to *teach* children, not let them play, need skill in naming what is learned through play.

Elena, a student teacher in kindergarten, was reluctant to take the initiative in leading activities until her supervising teacher picked up on her mention of making tortillas with the children. The tortilla making was a spectacular success, as edible curriculum often is. A parent brought salsa; another parent brought the ingredients for guacamole; and one child was highly motivated to read the recipe out loud, figuring out unfamiliar words from their context, as all sensible readers do. Lunch was lovely, and Elena, beaming from all the acknowledgment she received, kept discovering for herself that tortilla making isn't just fun; it's curriculum. "Oh, it's math! Oh, it's reading! Oh, it's science! Oh!"

Teachers who have discovered contextual curriculum for themselves are able to name it for others with a stake in the children's learning—parents, supervisors, and community members. We owe these people *representations* of children's significant understandings. Using oral and written language, drawings and photographs, teachers can use the same skills they're busy teaching to children, in order to provide a window into the action in our classrooms. If representation is what young children are busy practicing in school, *documentation* is what their teachers need to be practicing (Jones, Evans, & Rencken, 2001, p. 132).

And grownups do ask children what they did in school today. A teacher can give children—even 5-year-old English-language learners—the words for talking about their learning, both for their own self-awareness and for responding satisfactorily when Uncle Kao asks, "What do they teach you in that school?"

To have each child consider how he or she had grown as a writer over the year, I reviewed each portfolio with the individual child, [asking] "What do you think of yourself as a writer now?"

Yang: I like writing, because it is fun. I write by myself. Before I cannot write my name. I write my name. I write what I see.

Nai: I am a good writer. I can write a lot of words. I can tell stories about my friends. I want to write a silly story.

Cindy: I can read what I write.

Sarn: I like writing because [it is] to think. (Jones, Evans, & Rencken, 2001, pp. 73–74)

Teachers who use conventional names for learning activities and share those names with children are engaging in savvy public relations. Naming is part of being smart.

7

The Drama of Opposites: Good Guys, Bad Guys

Assumption: **We can outwit *Them*.**

"Aunt Sarah" played a tremendous role in my growing up. Aunt Sarah wasn't a person, it was a game that the entire neighborhood got involved in at one time or another—one of those crazy serialized games that just kind of appear. Nobody thinks it up. Nobody says "Hey, let's play Aunt Sarah." It's just *there* one afternoon.

The basic premise of Aunt Sarah (and it was always called that, very solemnly) was that we were running away from our evil Aunt Sarah, often chased by her slavering bloodhounds. And that's it. We played this for several years! This premise was the kickoff for hundreds of wild adventures. (Read, 1993, p. 40)

CHILDREN—even very young children—understand the drama of opposites. In much of their play they invent action between good guys and bad guys, ensuring that they, the good guys, win. Children frequently lose, in the real world, in conflicts with adults. (Often, they *should* lose; adults really do know better.) But to maintain self-esteem and the capacity to solve problems thoughtfully, children also need to experience a "we" of caring support with some of the adults in their lives, including, wherever possible, their teachers. Playing out problems with adult support, children become more confident and more ingenious. They get smarter.

Let's digress a moment for some definitions. Eve Trook's definition of the uses of power in teaching has guided our thinking for a long time:

Power exercised ON a child means that the child has no real choice, i.e., the child is *oppressed.*

Power exercised FOR a child means that the child is provided experiences that contribute to the development of self-esteem and confidence that lead to power for the child, i.e., the child is *facilitated.*

64

Power exercised WITH a child means that teacher and child are equals learning together and the child acquires new power, i.e., the child and teacher are *liberated*.

The critical difference between FOR and WITH is teacher control. Power used FOR the child means the teacher is intentionally guiding, structuring, or supporting toward a goal. Power WITH the child means both teacher and child share a sense of wonder and are creating together. (Trook in Jones, 1983, p. 16; Jones, 1986, p. 79)

Learning how to provide support for children getting smarter, adults can practice two approaches:

Power WITH: Following children's lead—learning from them about the bad guys and monsters that threaten them. Becoming co-players.

Power FOR: Teaching them—inventing stories and games that embed what we want to teach them into their existing understandings.

(Power ON is also a necessary component of teaching. But it doesn't make children smarter.)

POWER WITH THE CHILDREN

"It's not a gun, teacher!"

Brandon, after digging himself a trench in the sand, has transformed his short-handled shovel into an automatic weapon and is loudly mowing down an invisible enemy. But knowing that teachers don't belong on battlefields, he is quick to reassure her. In bad-guys play, the kids will win every time. Like the National Rifle Association, they are fiercely protective of their right to bear arms. Confronted with teacher rules to the contrary, they simply go underground and continue their homeland defense. Make-believe play is their weapon against their real fear of dangers known and unknown.

Schools and child-care centers have good reasons for banning violent play. As an approach to problem solving, violence is too simplistic. The play often escalates into real hurting. But it is silly, if you're a grownup, to take on battles with children that you can't win. If you can't fight 'em, join 'em—with win/win strategies like these, in order to make good-guys-bad-guys play more complicated and less violent. Keep in mind that it's *play*, and so the lead remains with the children. If you want to join in, you have to be playful too.

What do you call a computer superhero?
A screensaver.

Respect Their Expertise

Children usually know more than their teachers do about Batman and Super-man, Ninjas and Star Wars, the Incredible Hulk and Spiderman. The cast of superheroes keeps changing, while teachers just get older. To join the club, you need to be curious and willing to learn. How? You can watch the shows. You can ask the children. You can use your social skills to try to get in.

A kindergarten teacher surrounded by Ninja Turtles watched an episode of the show and then took advantage of writing/drawing time in her class to make an awkward sketch of a turtle. Miguel took a look at it. "Who's that?"
　　"I was trying to draw one of the Turtles," she told him.
　　"Which one?" he asked.
　　"I'm not sure. Is one of them called Donaldo?"
　　"No, Donatello," he said impatiently. "And you have to color his head thing blue, and you have to put his letter on his belt. Don't you know anything?"
　　"Is his letter *D*?" she guessed. "I know how to make a *D*."
　　"Do you? Show me," said Miguel eagerly.
　　"Like this," volunteered David, joining them. And Turtles became a writing lesson, just like that—an unplanned bonus from the teacher's perspective.

Gaye Gronlund (1992), also a teacher, commented on a similar experience:

The children's active play seemed to change almost immediately after I shared my interest in "Turtle culture." . . . and as they chased each other on the playground [they yelled to me], "Jacob is Shredder and we're all Donatello chasing him." I could then respond in the correct lingo, "Cowabunga, Dudes!" (p. 23)

By now Turtles are passé, but here comes Spiderman:

Spiderman, Spiderman,
　　Does whatever a spider can.
　　"What *can* he do?" asks a teacher who really doesn't know.
　　"He has spidy sense!" whoops Sammy gleefully.
　　"What's spidy sense?" asks the teacher, and a long impromptu discus-sion with several children takes place on the spot. It seems to be something like cats' whiskers, she infers: how you feel what's around you. And since

she likes both spiders and cats, who knows what mutual interests might grow out of this one?

Complicate Their Interests Further

Carlsson-Paige and Levin, in *The War Play Dilemma* (1987) and other writings, have proposed complicating bad-guys-good-guys play as one strategy for supporting more balanced learning. Are there any baby bats in the Bat Cave? If you loaded your gun with glue instead of bullets, what would that do to the bad guys? Does Spiderman make webs? (This is a genuine question; the teacher knows a lot about what spiders do, but nothing about Spiderman. To join children in their play, it's important to be genuinely playful. Where do your play and the children's play connect with each other?)

> *Why do spiders spin webs?*
> *Because they don't know how to knit.*

What do the children know about spiders? Spiders' lives are full of prey and predators too, like Spiderman's. Could we make a spiderweb? What would we need to do that? Where's Little Miss Muffet in this mix? Why was she scared? Who's afraid of spiders? Who's afraid of Spiderman? If this falls flat because the children's real interest is in heroes, not spiders, another possible theme for mutual play will come along at any moment.

Believe in Their Worlds

Children with autism pose a different challenge; they are focused on avoiding connection rather than on confrontation. Can a teacher join in their private imaginative play, thereby making connection harder to resist?

As a preschool teacher, Claire met Emma. Emma attended special education preschool in the mornings and Claire's preschool class, for 2 years, in the afternoons. Her mornings followed a behavior-management plan; in the afternoons she was freer to choose her play. Intent on the drama of her own imaginary worlds, she didn't seek out relationships and did her best to avoid school routines.

Most children initiate play and conversations with others. Children who prefer their own worlds can become more outgoing if their own worlds are actively, playfully acknowledged by friendly others. Because Emma's imaginative world drew, as children's typically do, on stories and films shared with her family, and because these were familiar to Claire as well, teacher and child had a language in which to communicate. It wasn't necessary to impose school language on Emma at all times.

One chilly November day Claire glanced out the window and discovered that 4-year-old Emma had evaded small-group activities and was out in the adjacent play yard, systematically lifting her leg along the fence. She was naked. Claire joined her at once.

Claire: Emma!
Emma: I'm King Mufasa.
Claire: Emma, what are you doing?
Emma: I'm marking my territory.
Claire: Well, please stop, put on some fur covering, and wash your paws for snack.

And Emma, though by no means a compliant child, allowed herself to be helped into covering and washed her paws for snack—though it was not zebra. Crackers (Ritz, her favorite) are almost as good as zebra.

On a later date:

Emma (holding imaginary umbrella): Practically perfect in every way!
Claire: Mary Poppins, please close your umbrella. There's not room for it on the bus.

If you have a teacher who knows both Lion King and Mary Poppins as well as you do, and imaginatively joins your play in "We" mode, it is harder to ignore the teacher or be defiant. And if you have friends who want to play with you and who have observed your teacher's strategies, you may find it increasingly hard to stay in your private world:

As Jessica arrived at school, she saw her friend Emma and started happily talking to her. After a few minutes she realized that Emma wasn't paying attention. Jessica moved directly into Emma's field of vision, thrust her face into Emma's, and said scoldingly, "You spozed to look when I talking to you, Emma!"

Vivian Paley, another believer in the internal logic of children's fantasy and the possibility of joining in as a playful teacher, tells in *Bad Guys Don't Have Birthdays* (1988) the story of "Doll-corner smashie." Christopher, waving the Raggedy Andy doll and a handful of playdough, calls to his friend, "Barney, look at me. This guy's going smashie-poopie all over the room." As the playdough hits the floor, the teacher approaches cautiously, having encountered this game with these bad guys before. Deciding to try conciliation rather than Outraged Teacher, she recalls last week's game as Christopher squeals, "It's doll-corner smashie!"

"Oh, yes," [she says.] "I remember that from last week. There was a bad guy trying to come to your picnic, wasn't there? Is that what's happening now?"

Christopher still doubts my sincerity. He looks at the boys for support. "Mr. Nobody," he blurts out. "I'm Mr. Nobody."

. . . I look upon Mr. Nobody as a new sort of bad guy who has the power to ensnare the entire educational process by doing nothing. Come to think of it, he does a great deal; it is no mean feat to entertain a classroom of children and annoy the teacher all at once.

"Is that the same Mr. Nobody Barney puts in some of his stories?" I ask.

"Yeah, he goes plop, plop, and no one ever sees him, ha, ha."

"Maybe so, Christopher, but the playdough *can* be seen and it's a big mess. Fredrick, you were the wish fairy before. That's a helpful person. Why don't you help Christopher pick it up?"

Fredrick will not be trapped so easily. "I'm Mr. Nobody too," he tells me, and goes over to Christopher's side of the room.

"Well, then, let both Mr. Nobodys pick up the play dough."

Fredrick frowns. "But wait, teacher. If someone is invisible, how can they see the playdough if it's not invisible?"

Fredrick is about to turn a messy floor into a Socratic dialogue. Is he trying to distract me or does his question represent an honest inquiry into the logic of fantasy? (Paley, 1988, pp. 99–101)

The teacher decides to go along in good faith, and a serious discussion follows, in an effort to use Mr. Nobody's invisibleness to solve a real classroom management problem. Fredrick finally figures it out: "'Pretend *everybody* is invisible in this room, even the teacher. Then if everyone is invisible it means the whole doll corner is invisible. See? Then the playdough *has* to be invisible. And we can pick it up.'" (p. 101).

And they do.

POWER FOR THE CHILDREN: ADDING OURS TO THEIRS

Working supportively with young children, a teacher needs to practice becoming bilingual and bicognitive. Helpful adults do this intuitively with a baby who is beginning to talk; we converse in *his* language, rather than expecting him to move directly into ours. "Da!" says the baby. "Da!" Mum responds, with a delighted hug and nuzzle. That's power WITH—playfully responding to the child's cue.

Power FOR kicks in when Daddy comes home. "Da!" says Junior, still going strong with this fine new sound. "Da da!"

"Dada!" exclaims Daddy, tossing him happily in the air. "Did you hear that? He said Daddy! Hey kid, can you say Daddy? Dad-dy." "Da-da-da-da-da!" says Junior, not to be outdone.

Scaffolding has begun. It will continue throughout language learning, as adults build on the child's initiative by leading him into the *zone of proximal development* (Vygotsky, 1978), helping him do what he can't quite do for himself yet. Learning to talk, walk, climb stairs—these are all skills that emerge directly out of the toddler's own initiative, supported by a responsive adult. Learning is *embedded* in desire, in previously discovered patterns, and in caring relationships.

Gwen Piper, an Early Head Start home visitor, tried modeling a responsive-language strategy for the young mother of an unusually silent 10-month old:

The baby is sitting silently in her mother's lap. I lean over and look at her and say, "Da da da." She says back to me, "Da da da." I laugh and we go more rounds, with full eye contact and engagement.

I explain this circle of communication to Mom, who says, "You know, this morning at 4 A.M. she was saying Nanananana, and I said 'Nononononono, you go to sleep.' You mean, she was talking to me? Wow—she was so happy. No wonder she was so happy, she thought I was talking to her!" (Piper, 2005, pp. 73–74)

All the teachers in the teacher-child stories we've been telling here were practicing bilingual and bicognitive skills as they learned the children's Turtle and Spiderman languages, reminded the Lion King to cover her fur, and struggled to understand the logic of an invisible Mr. Nobody. They granted power to the children as the authorities in this play.

But then there is school.

THE USES OF POWER IN SCHOOLS

School, for many children, is a *disembedded* experience—a new game with new rules and perhaps a whole new language as well. As children become more complex thinkers, they can benefit from explanations of the power structure. People who have power, as adults do over children, usually don't name it. They just use it. Teachers can help by discussing the rules of the school game as just that—not absolutes, but made-up rules just like the rules of tag or kick-the-can. Thus they become interesting challenges to be met or even argued about. Are they fair? What could we do about them?

"OK," said Imani, teacher and born cheerleader, to her second-grade class. "The principal of this school—what's his name? Oh yes, of course, Mr. Spalding. Mr. Spalding, he really cares about neat lines. I don't know why, but he does. Maybe that's what he learned when he was in second grade. We really don't want him to be mad at us, do we? He's the principal. He's the big boss at this school. So let's show him we can make the neatest, sharpest lines in the whole school. We're going to practice right now.

"Line up! Make it straight! Straighter! . . . Pull in that elbow! Look straight at the back of the neck in front of you. March, in place! Faster! . . . Halt! (Know what that means? It means Stop!) Try it again—Halt! wow! Give yourselves a hand!"

Imani is not only training her 7-year-olds to obey the rules about lining up at Third Street School; she is also letting them in on the challenge *We* face in getting along with *Them*—the people who make and enforce the rules. In Lisa Delpit's (1995) words, she is teaching them about the *culture of power*. As their ally (who doesn't personally care very much about neat lines, even though she's one of the grownups), she's creating an opportunity for dramatic action and outwitting the enemy.

Don't sweat the small stuff, she's teaching them. Children even in preschool have learned that grownups think lots of things are important that aren't. Usually it's more sensible to humor them than to argue— and then play Meany Mommy or Bad Guys with the other kids. Cool teachers can model this attitude, with a sense of fun, and demonstrate survival strategies.

That's not common teacher behavior; most teachers aren't trying to be cool. There is, instead, a very long school tradition of intimidating new children through distancing from the adult, incomprehensible rules and, historically, corporal punishment. (If you're a reader of novels, look for Meggie's first day of school in *The Thorn Birds* [McCullough, 1977, p. 26].) In milder form, I (Betty) watched a kindergarten teacher's distancing behavior in our neighborhood school, as she decisively erected barriers between the familiar and the new. ("The children must learn that kindergarten is not nursery school," she said firmly to me in a parent conference.) Although English was not the first language of perhaps half the children, she began by changing children's names—from Jorge to George, Rosa Maria to Rose Marie, and Isolina ("Oh, that's not an American name. We'll call you Hazel"). The teacher was herself a native Spanish speaker, but she spoke Spanish in the classroom only to scold those children who might miss her meaning in English.

This happened a generation ago, and perhaps schools have become more benign, more attuned to young children's needs for continuity and caring in order for them to build trust in themselves as learners. However, there has been a steady increase in the ultimate distancing strategy—standardized testing.

What do you get when you cross a vampire with a teacher?
A blood test.

Testing as Trickery

When my (Betty's) son was studying for the Graduate Record Exam, he had an *aha*: "They're all trick questions." Of course, that's part of the plot. To ensure a reasonable proportion of failures, a good test is rigorous; that is, it is designed to weed out the failures from the successes. To produce more wrong answers, tests use, not one, but two, strategies for assessing test-takers' knowledge. The first is straightforward: Do you know this fact, this process, this answer? The other, especially characteristic of multiple-choice tests, is tricky: You'll get caught if you don't think twice about the difference between item b and item c, which is worded to catch you if it can. Not only knowledge, but also alertness to nuance, is being tested.

Testers of children use a third strategy that invites failure: a setting in which all the usual help and comfort is missing. Standardized testing, a school ritual increasingly imposed even on 4-year-olds, requires teachers to be bad guys who follow every step in the sacred ritual. During testing, a teacher accustomed to offering friendly support and helpful hints to her first graders is suddenly required to be distant and silent, to pretend (absurdly) that she has no relationship with the children. The threatening atmosphere thus created, perhaps not incidentally, helps to weed out those children who are too trusting and too dependent. "High stakes" testing serves as a rite of passage, as artificial and stilted and scary as it can be. Keep a stiff upper lip and do your best.

What do you get if you cross a vampire and a snowman?
Frostbite.

Where this ritual has been elevated to become the determinant of school funding, teacher pay, and even housing prices, it is no wonder that some school personnel make efforts to undermine it. Good-guy teachers who help kids improve their scores are, however, publicly denounced as cheaters. Even in the newspapers.

Interestingly, Piaget, in his famous studies of what young children understand, bought into the distancing approach completely. Coming from a rational/scientific tradition that insists on "objectivity," he dismissed both "romance" and relationships as interferences in his study of children. "One would like to be able to rule out romancing with the same severity as [those answers designed to please the questioner]," he wrote (Piaget, 1951, p. 10). The child, then, was told in effect: "Don't make things up. Don't pay attention to me. Just *THINK*."

But why? What is the point of the game this big person wants me to play? Children's knowing is embedded in imagination—stories—and relationships. Piaget didn't want his subjects to think up answers to please the questioner. But why else would they bother to do the task? When there's no meaning, children look carefully at the adult's face to see if they're on the right track. Unless a situation of shared meaning is constructed, what motivation is available to children, in testing and in compulsory education in general, other than avoidance of punishment and hope of acknowledgment?

The testing game, from a child's perspective, is about good guys and bad guys. The kids, naturally, are the good guys, and those bad guys are out to trick us and catch us. The adult with children facing this situation can take either of two roles: aloof bad guy (like Piaget) or helpful good guy (cheater?). Another researcher, free from the rules of the standardized testers, tried the helpful-good-guy approach and—surprise!—the children she tested turned out to be much smarter than Piaget's.

EMBEDDED VS. DISEMBEDDED KNOWING

About 25 years after Piaget's research, one of the Piagetian tasks that Margaret Donaldson (1978) and her associates reinvented was an investigation of children's "perspective-taking." Piaget used a model of three mountains, placed on a table in front of the child. "What do you see?" The experimenter then shows the child a little doll, which he places on the table at the other side of the mountains. "What does the doll see?"

Young children failed to recognize the doll's perspective as different from their own, thus supporting Piaget's theory of their inability to decenter. Skeptical of this interpretation, Donaldson's research team imaginatively tried a similar task with two crucial differences: the question was embedded in a bad-guys-good-guys story, and the tester was not impersonal, but helpful.

It began with two "walls" intersecting to form a cross, and two small dolls identified as a policeman and a little boy. The child was introduced to the task "very carefully, in ways that were designed to give him every chance of understanding the situation fully and grasping what is being asked of him. . . . The child was asked to 'hide the doll so that the policeman can't see him'" (pp. 13–14).

Very few mistakes were made. Even as the task was increased in difficulty by adding more policemen, 90% of four-year-olds' responses were correct. Donaldson writes:

It is difficult to avoid the conclusion that the children who make "egocentric" responses to the "mountains" problem do not fully understand what they are supposed to do. By contrast, it is quite evident that in the "policeman" problem a situation has been found which *makes sense* to the child. . . . the children seemed to grasp the situation at once. We have then to ask why this was so easy for them.

Notice that we cannot appeal to direct actual experience: few, if any, of these children had ever tried to hide from a policeman. But we *can* appeal to the generalization of experience; they know what it is to try to hide. Also they know what it is to be naughty and to try to evade the consequences. So that they can easily conceive that a boy might want to hide from a policeman if he had been a bad boy: for in this case it would be the job of the policeman to catch him and the consequences of being caught would be undesirable.

The point is that the *motives* and *intentions* of the characters are entirely comprehensible, even to a child of three. The task requires the child to act in ways which are in line with certain very basic human purposes and interactions (escape and pursuit)—it makes *human sense*. . . . in this context he shows none of the difficulty in "decentering" which Piaget ascribes to him.

[Piaget's mountains task, like standardized testing,] is abstract in a psychologically very important sense: in the sense that it is abstracted from all basic human purposes and feelings and endeavors. It is totally cold-blooded. In the veins of three-year-olds, the blood still runs warm. (pp. 16–17)

Piaget's task invites few associations, no pleasure in humor. In contrast, the policeman evokes smiles of recognition: How clever of the experimenter to create a story that engages the child's feelings and motives! Imagination is what's needed as the child, who knows all about naughty, is invited into the game posed by the story: Can you help the frightened little doll hide from the policeman? Imagining is what young children are good at doing, and so they get the test answers right after all.

This is in no way to suggest that the ability to deal, in cold blood, with problems of an abstract and formal nature is unimportant. It is immensely important. Much that is distinctively human and highly to be valued depends on it. And young children are bad at it. (Donaldson, 1978, pp. 17–18)

Working with young children, one can focus on what they're bad at and try to fix them. Or one can focus on what they're good at and engage with them as Vygotsky suggested—*scaffolding* new experiences within the context of their current interests and understanding. The latter produces *embedded* knowing. As Vivian Paley (1988) reminds us, that's what young children are masters of. At the end of the "doll-corner smashie" story told earlier, Christopher hugs his teacher "as hard as he can. He loves it when I behave sensibly," she explains. The whole sequence of events, from throwing playdough to pondering the implications of invisibility, has been transformed into "motivations for telling a story, which is what children know how to do best" (p. 102).

Sense, for young children, is emotional and narrative. It is embedded in the connections of their past experience. Ordinary living, for all of us, takes place in the context of personal meaning. Formal schooling is different; it is preparation for life in a society which places the highest value on thinking that is abstracted from personal meaning. This is the kind of thinking required by science and mathematics and engineering and the running of bureaucracies. In Donaldson's (1978) words, "The better you are at tackling problems without having to be sustained by human sense, the more likely you are to succeed in our educational system" (pp. 77–78).

Parents who pressure preschool teachers to *teach* their children are aware of this, and so they are reassured by the presence of worksheets in the classroom. That's real school—meaningless to the children, perhaps, but familiar to the grownups as "the way it spozed to be." Uncowed children may keep insisting on meaning, on making sense of their experience. Thus, a child taking an achievement test responded to a paragraph about a boy named Tom: "I have a friend named Tom and he doesn't do that."

Abstract logic is not a good model for teaching young children. It treats "young children as fools" (Egan, 1986, p. 18) by ignoring their capacity for imaginative thinking, which develops very early indeed. As children move into elementary school, ready to become "serious players" (Wasserman, 2000) of games with rules and investigators of all sorts of phenomena (Gallas, 1995), we can keep their learning embedded in meaning by revealing the rules of the game—thus staying firmly on the side of the good guys, that is, us.

In *Teaching as Storytelling*, Kieran Egan (1986) writes:

What we call imagination is also a tool of learning—in the early years perhaps the most energetic and powerful one. [Our focus has been directed] by the dominant forms of research on those skills children are least good at. . . . If we continue to keep imaginative intellectual activity as our focus we might be able to construct a more hopeful and less constrictive image of the child as learner. Such an image would, it seems to me, be more in keeping with our everyday experience of children's intellectual energy than is the Piagetian view of relative intellectual incompetents. This is not to say that we will ignore what children seem typically unable to do, but rather than we will focus on what they most obviously *can* do, and seem able to do best. (pp. 17, 21–22)

There really are bad guys out there—in the flesh, and in the recesses of the mind. Exorcism is a ritual taken seriously by grownups in many traditions; by driving away invisible evils, it restores balance and puts the good guys back in charge. If we are on the children's side, we can support their imaginations in order to keep them safe and confident.

"See? Then the playdough has to be invisible. And then we can pick it up." Playing, children get smart.

What did the cat say when it got hurt?
Me-ow.

What happens when a cat eats a lemon?
It becomes a sour puss.

CAT TO CAT: *People are OK, but I prefer small bits of string.*

8

Peacemaking:
Letting the Bad Guys Go

Assumption: **We can practice caring for *Them*. And we should, because peacemaking is safer (though less exciting) than making war.**

What do you call a fight between bats?
A battle.

What do you call wildebeests that won't behave?
Bad gnus.

One kid: Who gave you that black eye?
Other kid: Nobody. I had to fight for it.

WHEN we practice outwitting bad guys, we have cheerfully identified them as the enemy. They're the folks who get in our way, who won't let us do what we want and need to do. They're wrong, we're right—but we don't have to say so out loud. Our challenge is to avoid trouble while getting our way. Caring adults can help children learn to think this way.

That is the *doubting game* as played by those not in power. While *They* tell us the rules, *We* think critically about those rules: Are they sensible? Fair? Do they apply to us? What will the consequences be if we don't follow them? Critical thinking is a very important skill, an asset for the citizen in a democracy. Our own revolutionary history teaches us that rules made by tyrants should be overthrown. Some teachers really are unreasonable tyrants, trying to break children's spirit. Those children need allies, from among their peers and even from among the caring adults in their lives. They need to practice critical thinking.

But this chapter is about the move from doubt to belief, in search of empathy even for *Them*.

Sneaking is a sensible strategy under circumstances in which the tyrants aren't likely to go away. Very young children, whom Piaget described as being unable to hold two concepts in their heads at the same time, may not be ready to take it very far (though as we saw in the preceding chapter, Piaget underestimated what children can do with their imagination). School-age children, however, not only can master this strategy but also may gradually develop the insights that lead toward empathy and peacemaking, as this 10-year-old has:

The children came in angry after recess, complaining about the mean yard teacher who had yelled at them. Their teacher, a master peacemaker with a clearly established structure for collective problem solving, invited them to discuss their concerns. "Is there anything you could do about it?" she asked after they had vented their feelings and mention had been made of the difficulty of the yard teacher's job (on a large, poorly equipped school playground).
    "Maybe we could sweet-talk her," said Danny, thoughtfully.
    "Do you think that would make her nice?" asked the teacher, genuinely curious.
    "Probably not," said Danny. "But it might make her nicer to *us*."

Danny is engaged not only in critical thinking but also in the practice of empathy—the *believing game*. To practice caring is harder, and less satisfyingly dramatic, than outwitting enemies. How, we ask, could anyone believe *that*? Why might anyone behave that way? Is there a win/win solution, perhaps, in which no one will get hurt? To find it, a change of perspective is required: How can we get what we want *and* how can they get what they want?

> *He drew a circle that shut me out—*
> *Heretic, rebel, a thing to flout.*
> *But Love and I had the wit to win:*
> *We drew a circle that took him in.*
>   Edwin Markham

CONFLICT RESOLUTION AS CURRICULUM

Empathy does not, perhaps, come as easily to the young, at least among humans and other carnivores, as the wielding of tooth and claw. But it can be systematically taught from early childhood on, by grownups who value the acquisition of conflict-resolution skills, even among toddlers.

A thoughtful educarer observes from close range as a large red ball rolls across the floor of the playroom. The 10-month-old who batted it in that direction is crawling rapidly after it, but it is scooped up by an artful walker several months older. The baby cries, indignantly. "Baw!" she demands loudly. The ball's new possessor sits down abruptly but holds on tightly. He tries to push the crawler away. The observing adult joins them on the floor, with a gentle hand on each. "You want the ball," she says clearly to the crawler. "And you want the ball," she says to the toddler. "What can we do, I wonder?" She reaches out with her foot to snag another ball—a yellow one—nearby on the floor. "Would someone like this ball?"

For preverbal children not yet ready to negotiate sharing, providing more than one of a desired object is the most caring solution. As children move into effective language, the adult encounters the basic 1- and 2-year-old claim of "Mine!"—one of the most important words in a young child's vocabulary in the stage of *autonomy* (exercise of the will to get what one wants).

Patty has brought her new stuffed lion to visit child care. "Oh, Patty, what a nice lion," says the teacher. "Is it new?"

"Mine," says Patty happily, showing it to the teacher. Bob stops playing and watches for a moment. Then he reaches out and grabs the lion's tail.

"No!" says Patty. "My wion!" Bob pulls harder. Patty hits him.

The teacher intervenes. "It isn't nice to hit. Bob likes your lion. Could you let him hold it?"

"No!" says Patty, hitting Bob again.

"You need to use your words," says the teacher.

(Patty *is* using her words; she's just backing them up with her fist.) Bob won't let go of the tail. Patty screams. The teacher, looking increasingly anxious, pries Bob's fingers away from the tail and, fending him off with one arm, suggests hopefully to Patty that perhaps Lion can take a nap in her cubby. "No!" says Patty. *My wion!"*

Wars have been fought for less.

A teacher of 3-year-olds writes that she has gained in confidence about intervening in conflicts as she has

learned to gear my interactions toward helping children communicate with each other, knowing that children enjoy playing together. When they have a hard time doing so, it is often because they need help figuring out the perspective of the other person.

For example, one day I stopped two boys running and chasing each other around the gym to ask if they were having a problem, or if they were playing a game, because I couldn't be sure. Based on what they told me, I figured out that they had been chasing each other because they both wanted to use the same basketball and not surprisingly, they each only wanted to use *that* ball even though there were many similar balls available. The two boys and I were unable to figure out who had the ball first, or how it came to be that they both thought they had the ball first, and they each wanted me to give the ball back to them. Not knowing myself how best to resolve their dilemma, I explained that if I gave the ball to one of them, then the other would be disappointed. I admitted to them that I didn't know the best way to work out their problem fairly. I asked them if they couldn't together figure out a way for them to both use the ball. I don't know exactly how long we sat together on the mats, while no one said anything. All of a sudden, one of the boys jumped up with a look of "a-ha" on his face and said, "I know, we can share the ball!"

A couple of days later, I helped the same two boys work out a similar problem with a hockey puck. From then on, their preference was to play together, calling it "real" basketball or "real" hockey. Things like passing and taking turns became important parts of their game. (Moore, 1998, pp. 132–133)

Isn't that obvious? Not if you're 3 and are in between "Mine!" and "Will you be my friend and play with me?" Given time to construct under-standing for oneself, and adult support in doing so, friendship is pretty sure to win out.

By age 4, children who have had lots of practice have this script down pat. They also know how time-consuming it is.

Two children had begun squabbling over possession of a new sand toy, a large shiny bucket. Voices were raised, fists were lifted—and an alert teacher moved toward the scene, ready to mediate problem solving. Knowing what was coming, the little girl said impatiently, "Oh no, I don't want to problem solve. I've got to fix dinner for the babies. He can have it. I'll get something else."

A teacher-as-mediator may deflect conflict simply by asking a pro-vocative question that makes the play more interesting and invites collaboration.

We got some new shovels a couple of weeks ago, which stimulated renewed interest in digging. I was out there by the sand one day when tempers were rising; the conflict was territorial. I tried a challenge: "How far down in the earth do you think you can dig?" The idea really grabbed them. "You'll get there faster if you work as a team," I said. The group dynamics improved instantly, and they pursued their common goal with much discussion.

One girl thought they could go as far as the devil.

Another thought they'd get to China.

Another mentioned that he didn't think they'd get very far because the walls would cave in.

All the while they dug, and at the end of the day someone said they should measure the hole and keep a record. They've been measuring everything in sight ever since. (Jones & Nimmo, 1994, p. 121)

By ages 4 and 5, some skillful sociodramatic players show clear evidence of empathy as they enlarge the play circle to include all interested comers. Here's Maria, in effective charge of the action in the sandbox, wielding her power for the general good:

She was making sand cakes for a party, molding damp sand in a shallow cup, and turning it carefully onto a plank table, then decorating each cake with a sprinkling of leaves, twigs, and a sprinkling of dry sand. She dealt skillfully with a series of potential interruptions: a boy who wanted to eat a cake ("No, the party hasn't started yet, but I'll save that one for you."), another girl who wanted to make a bigger cake with a pie pan ("We need them all the same size at this party. Use this cup."), and an accident with a passing truck that demolished part of a cake ("That one wasn't very good anyway. Here, put the rest of it in your truck and I'll make a new one.") At last the party really took place, with several satisfied celebrants. (Jones, 1986, pp. 62–63)

Clearly, Maria has had lots of modeling and practice with "Use your words," and her behavior provides remarkable evidence of playing to get smart.

The believing game (introduced in Chapter 1) is most effectively played, and taught, by those who do have power. For the powerless, it too rapidly becomes acquiescence. For those with a secure place, self-confidence, and curiosity about the nuances of friendship, it's an empowering tool of great importance in human civility. The teacher of young children, puzzled by behavior she doesn't understand, asks herself the believing question, "Why would a child behave this way?" The teacher challenged by subversion of classroom order must either become tyrannical or develop strategies for creating a caring classroom community. An inclusive community isn't necessarily children's goal, given their investment in the drama of bad guys–good guys. Its creation demands lots of problem solving.

CREATING CLASSROOM COMMUNITY

In early childhood programs with more than one adult present and children small enough to pick up and hold as needed, classroom control isn't a constant issue. Children aren't often required to sit still and be quiet; they can be the active learners their bodies insist that they be. In "real school," however, where one adult has sole responsibility for a large group of increasingly savvy young persons, control is everyone's first priority. In the tradition of schooling, learning is equated with sitting quietly and listening or writing. Primary teacher and teacher-researcher Karen Gallas (1998) has written:

I still feel bad for the boys who walk into my classroom as first graders. I know that their lives, as they have known them, are about to end. Inside the school and within a classroom, these poor, once carefree children have to be "civilized." They can't run, wrestle, roll, push, spit, hit, or produce bloodcurdling screams.

As their teacher, I have to help them begin to contain themselves. It is a sad sight to see when they realize what's happening. Some of them immediately rebel, and . . . continue to rebel at every possible opportunity. Others are able to accept my authority and the reasons I give them to justify their containment, but it hurts them. . . . sitting long enough to hear a story can be a form of torture. (pp. 26–27)

Gallas is among the creative teachers who ingeniously work to include the children, resistant though some of them may be, in the process of community building. She shares John Dewey's (1964) conviction that the human need for connection with others is sufficient motivation for children to welcome guidance toward mature social skills.

Such guidance is not preprogrammed. It happens most effectively when observant teachers create opportunities for conversation and group discussion that enable children to participate fully in collective problem solving. Here is an excerpt from a long discussion in a prekindergarten class. Peter and Eileen are the teachers.

(The children have just played a game. One child, Marissa, is nearly crying because of something that happened in the game and Peter wants to ask about this.) Peter: How many people got caught in that game? Hold up your hands. Look around, look how many people got caught. You know why I'm asking that? To show you how many people got caught. Sometimes you get caught, sometimes you don't. So when somebody does get caught, you don't have to make them feel bad because a lot of people got caught.
    (Lively conversation about catching ensues. Peter interrupts.)

Peter: Wait. Marissa, did you have a question about what we were talking about?

Marissa: Somebody catched me and they maked fun of me.

(*More conversation follows, about who caught Marissa and what they said. Eileen interrupts.*)

Eileen: Timothy, wait a second. I think Luke had something to say about this, about why he said something to her. He said he was the line judge and that's why he told you that he got caught.

Marissa: I don't like it.

Eileen: What didn't you like about it?

Marissa: I don't want him to do that. I don't want anybody to do that.

Timothy: Yeah but that . . .

Luke: That's what's gonna happen.

(*More conversation erupts.*)

Eileen: Let me ask a question about the line judge. Does the line judge tell everybody when they get caught, or does the line judge have to tell when it's really close to see if people made it over the line or didn't make it over the line? What's the job of a line judge?

Benjamin: The second one.

Eileen: The second one?

Peter: Only when it's a close call? Marissa, did you know that you were caught?

Marissa: Yes.

Peter: Well, Marissa, when the line judge told you that you got caught, did he say it just to let you know, or did he say it in a way that was like calling you names?

(*There is a long silent pause.*)

Peter: Or was it hard to tell?

Marissa: The second part.

Eileen: Did you feel like you were getting teased?

(*Marissa nods.*)

Timothy: Hey Marissa, sometimes that happens to me when my sister calls me a name. I'm upset.

Marissa (more animated): My sister always calls me names.

Timothy: Yeah, me too.

Anne: My brother always calls me names . . . *And lots of other kids have something to say too.*

(Moore, 1998, pp. 72–74)

Caring has taken over, as skillful teacher guidance succeeds in moving the discussion from complaints to empathy toward discovery of common experiences at home as well as at school.

THE ART OF SUSTAINING CONFLICT

John Nimmo tells this story from Reggio Emilia, Italy:

(Elisa, age 3, has created something flat and circular with playdough, carefully arranging toothpicks on it and asking the assistant to "light" her candles. Tomasso is watching.)

With a look of considerable certainty he states, *"Es una dolce"* [This is a cake]. Elisa corrects [him]: *"No es una dolce. Es una pizza"* [This is *not* a cake. This is a pizza].

The interaction proceeds between them in alternate volleys something like this: *No. Si. No. Si. No. Si. No! Si! No!* Each response is louder and more definitive than the last. . . . *"una dolce! una dolce!"* (We find out later that Tomasso's grandmother runs a pizzeria.) The teacher asks, "Tomasso, are you sure?" But his attention remains with Elisa. Again: *NO, una pizza. No. Si. No. Si. No. Si. No. Si. No!*

[Time passes. The argument goes on. Finally,]

After a long minute of silence Tomasso leaves, and the teacher sits at the table to take Elisa's dictation about her work. Elisa is very particular about what the teacher writes; she deliberates carefully and points to her words on the paper. Elisa says, *"Es una pizza."* And after a pause of reflection, she suddenly lunges forward and exclaims with certainty, *"Ma dolce, dolce* [But sweet, sweet!]!" The word for cake and sweet in the Italian language is the same: *dolce.*

Nimmo goes on to point out that the story of Elisa and Tomasso

is an example of provocation and the resulting co-construction of knowledge at possibly its very earliest appearance—at least in verbal language. This is no compromise. Elisa shaped a new idea—"sweet pizza"—from her conflict with Tomasso. Collaboration involves more than a coming together. It requires more from the participants than simply sharing their perspectives. At best, it requires that the participants reach a new level of understanding—a perspective that was not apparent before. (Jones & Nimmo, 1999, p. 6)

Make pizza, not war.

Conflict maintenance can build friendships. It can create new ideas and win/win solutions. Or, alternatively, it can create feuds that go on from generation to generation, providing drama and sometimes victory for those in power and, often, hardship for everyone else. The Martins and the Coys ("they were reckless mountain boys," went the pop song of my [Betty's] childhood), England's Yorks and Lancasters and the clan chiefs who appear, from the historical notes in Scottish castles today, to have warmed themselves up every dank winter by attacking their neighbors—a pattern repeated in both cold and warm climes all over the world—all exemplify world history told as a series of wars: bad guys–good guys drama.

Some battles take place over silly things ("Una pizza! Una dolce!"), but it all depends on one's perspective. Territorial wars between grownup armies are heightened greatly in passion if each side claims the territory as holy ground. Mythmaking, practiced in the play of early childhood and reinforced these days by media games of bad guys–good guys, is much more often focused on good and evil than on peacemaking. Good and evil provide action drama, enlivening the day-to-dayness of making a living. Only saints and other idealists can make drama out of peacemaking, and Terminators are still more readily popular heroes.

Territory is a reality base for struggle when there's a drought going on and our land isn't providing enough grass for our sheep. Your grasslands are better than ours and you're right next door and if we fight you for them and win, then our sheep will thrive (and we can add your sheep to them, and dress warmer and eat better). Animals, even herbivores, fight one another for territory. That's survival. What human beings do is manufacture stories to justify it all—playful behavior that they first practiced in their preschool years. Back in our great-grandfathers' time the evil king in the lands across the river made war upon our people . . . It's the family feud writ large, and it's carried on across the generations partly for the drama of it and partly to distract the people from overthrowing their leaders in protest because the sheep are dying. To be a war leader is to be heroic and noble, in ancient times and even today. War leaders don't get voted out of office, because we need them to protect us in these dangerous times. The threat of enemies, real or imagined, helps to coalesce national spirit and make everyone behave according to the rules of our—the good guys'—society.

THE ART OF FORGIVENESS

In *Fiddler on the Roof*, Tevye, "the Papa" struggling to understand his changing world, comments with rueful wisdom:

> An eye for an eye, a tooth for a tooth.
> That's justice.
> And it leaves everyone blind and toothless.

To appreciate and respect diversity, we have to find and share the stories that serve as a point of connection between us and not-us.

When I think differences can never be bridged, I remind myself of President Jimmy Carter's negotiating a peace agreement between two archenemies. President Carter created a safe, nonjudgmental space of wonderment for the leaders of two warring powers, Israel and Egypt, to find common ground. Anwar Sadat and Menachem Begin carried the scars of centuries of *jihad*. Sadat and Begin did not want to be in the same room, and certainly not at the same side of the table.

Something inspired President Carter to invite each man to talk about his grandchildren. "Tell us about them, what they are like, what they love, what they want to be," encouraged Carter. Slowly the stiffly defended men softened into gentle, beaming grandfathers with endless stories of delight. In the end, leaders Sadat and Begin agreed that the world should be a safer, saner place for their grandchildren than it had been for them. The peace accord was signed. A humble President Carter added his own cultural history in announcing the accord: "In my religious heritage, we say 'blessed are the peacemakers.'" (Bruno, 2003, p. 59)

Forgiveness takes much more imagination than revenge does. Revenge is a matter of simple justice—he hurt me, I'll hurt him. Imagination and creative problem solving are practiced in play and sustained in faith that things could be different, that aikido is a better idea than karate, that behaving in ways that surprise might disarm the enemy. There is, of course, no guarantee. But Gandhi imagined it, King imagined it, Chavez imagined it, Mandela and Tutu imagined it. Let us forgive the unforgivable. Let us try to believe that there is human goodness, buried somewhere deep, in those soldiers, police, terrorists, politicians, mean teachers, rowdy children. As we practice caring for them, we might save ourselves as well. Hate destroys the hater as well as the hated. War inevitably creates atrocities on all sides.

In a world that has so largely engaged in a mad and often brutally harsh race for material gain by means of ruthless competition, it behooves the school to make ceaseless and intelligently organized effort to develop above all else the will for co-operation and the spirit which sees in every other individual one who has an equal right to share in the cultural and material fruits of collective human invention, industry, skill and knowledge. (Dewey, 1940, p. 298)

THE POLITICS OF ENJOYMENT

Without boredom and anxiety, war would not be needed. Yet schooling works hard at accustoming children to both boredom and anxiety, in the name of discipline and learning. Is that necessary? In his book *Beyond Boredom and Anxiety* (1975) Mihaly Csikszentmihalyi has written about "the politics of enjoyment." Educators, he says, must assist children to

> recognize opportunities for action in an environment—teaching children what they can do with their bodies, with their fingers, and with their mind. A child trained to develop all the skills of his body and his mind need never feel bored or helpless and therefore alienated from his surroundings. (pp. 204–205)

Steinman (2004), in reviewing a book by James Hillman, a Jungian analyst, asks:

> Could the same intensity of engagement that is brought to war-making be directed to a positive, equally life-changing force? Are there other ways, Hillman writes, "for civilization to normalize martial fury . . . and open to the sublime?"
> "If every young person had an intense, passionate interest in making something, in groups or alone, in which they were engaged with their gut and their blood and their heart and their soul—in which it's a life-or-death struggle—as anyone knows who tries to work at something with passionate intensity, would that be an 'aesthetic equivalent of war'?" he asks. At a time when arts education has been all but eliminated from school budgets, it's a startling concept. (p. E4)

Education, in its root meaning ("to draw out"), seeks to engage that passionate interest. It exists in all children, unless it is smothered. Sylvia Ashton-Warner (1963), teaching young children, wrote about sustaining interest through the cycle of *breathing in* and *breathing out*. A child—any learner—has new experiences. She breathes them in. To make them truly her own, to construct her own understanding and skills, she needs extended time to breathe out, to practice, to assimilate—to play. Time to read stories—and to write her own stories. Time to look at great paintings, to try copying others' paintings—and to paint for herself. Time to watch a teacher inventing a math problem—and to join a small group of kids to invent their own math problems. Time to watch and listen to a teacher skilled in conflict resolution with children—and to try peacemaking with her peers.

We teach children what they're developmentally ready for. In early childhood that includes learning

Basic physical skills
Safety: Stay alert
Language and literacy

Classification of all sorts (this includes math)
Social problem solving—making and keeping friends and
    relationships
Choice-making

And all these things are learned through play.

What do you get when you cross a chicken with a millipede?
Drumsticks for everyone.

9

Play Across the Generations

What kind of stories do little ghosts tell around the campfire?
People stories.

What do cows read to their babies at bedtime?
Dairy tales.

A BABY, said William James, experiences the world as a big booming buzzing confusion. And so it is. Each of us spends a lifetime discovering and creating the patterns by which we live—friendships, words on paper, photographs of loved places and people, matching socks each morning. This task is the inevitable fate of an animal with a very large brain. The attention of simpler creatures is pre-wired; they aren't tempted to pay attention to *everything*. They don't play with possibilities. Whether they are sea anemones waving in a tide pool, sheep in a lush green meadow, or ants in your kitchen sink, they simply concentrate on food when it comes along.

Why is it hard to count sheep and cows?
Sheep are baa-d and cows keep moo-ving.

Human adults and older children never-endingly guide littler ones in what to attend to and what to leave alone. "I see you. Peekaboo." "No no, dirty!" "Shut your mouth, put both feet on the floor, and keep your eyes on your own paper." To learn important things like deciphering print, a child has to recognize the tiny differences between *d* and *b*, *p* and *q*, and the notion that e, E, Ë, ê, ε, Є, and *e* are all the same letter even when carelessly scribbled by a hasty note-writer.

Because so many boundaries aren't clear, it's no wonder that children get in trouble so often. However, they also get in trouble on purpose, playing "What will she do if I . . ?" a game mastered by most children before the end of their 2nd year. It's called teasing, and it's fun, even if risky.

Orderly patterns may be dictated or discovered. The dictators of order are preoccupied with safety—physical, social, and spiritual. Discoverers of order are engaging in play. Adult caregivers who engage in play, in their relationships with young children, are helping them to master play as a strategy for a lifetime of choice making. Play is an art; and "the arts teach children to exercise that most exquisite of capacities, the ability to make judgments in the absence of rules"(Eisner, 2005, p. B15; also see Eisner, 2002).

STAGE-SETTING: THE PHYSICAL ENVIRONMENT

As soon as crawlers crawl and toddlers toddle, they start to make messes. They dump, they pour, they knock over, they strew, they toss. These are all basic physical skills taken for granted by adults but essential to cooking, planting crops, construction, and many popular team games. Co-ordination requires endless practice. To encourage such practice, we can arrange an environment not too full of objects to practice on, easily visible and accessible to the very small.

On the edge of the low-walled sandbox in the toddler play yard are three dump trucks, one red, one blue, and one yellow. In the sand is an orderly array of four pails, two red with yellow handles, two yellow with red handles. Each pail is tipped on its side, with some sand in it. Each has a shovel matching its handle.

Not only the dumpers and diggers, but also the animal lovers are welcomed. Three groups of plastic animals—six horses, four cows—are also waiting in the sand.

To play requires the ability to choose. The littlest children can choose most easily if the *figure-ground relationships* are clear. Each morning, before they arrive, the staff sets up the environment to welcome the children—and delight their own eyes as well.

When the children arrive, they mess it up. It's the grownups' job to keep putting things back in order, cheerfully, so the babies can mess them up again. The more action, the more mess—and the more learning. It's awareness of the details of this learning that ensures that those who love toddlers remain cheerful learners themselves. "Did you see what Marcela just did?! Isn't she adorable, and smart?"

MEDIATING: THE PEER ENVIRONMENT

To be able to play with other children, young children need both civilizing and socializing. The civilized do not bite or crash sand pails on others' heads. They take someone's hand when it's time to cross the street. These are basic, dictated boundaries that enable us to relax in the presence of others. The socialized go beyond the basics; they are discovering how to make and keep a friend. Friends make play more interesting; they introduce new patterns and thus require negotiating skills. Adults and older children can teach those skills through modeling and conversations.

Three boys are building with the big blocks.
"This is our house, OK? Hey everybody, everybody. I'm making a door."
There is a selection of small animals on a shelf, and two of the boys begin playing with long wiggly snakes. They make a pile of "scary things—crocodile, vampire—" One boy crawls under a table, saying "Come on, brother, gimme my snake."
The other boy has continued building.

Builder: Mrs. Duke, come see our door.
Teacher: Is it safe for me to come in? Do I have to knock?
Boys: We got a snake!
(They roar at her.)
Teacher: I thought they were nice snakes.
Boys: They are. They don't bite.
Teacher: OK, then it's safe for me to come in.
Boys: These are the little snakes. This is the mama. This is the daddy.
They're nice.

(*A girl comes over to show Mrs. Duke her collage.*)

Teacher (to the boys): I'll be back to visit later, OK?

(*Suddenly the play is transformed.*)

I'm going to the store. I get some money.
Hey, rob the bank! Rob the bank, OK? (He goes off and comes back)
They gave us 50 dollars.
Put the cash in here.
No, we're the pet shop. We never steal, OK?
Let's go get the food. They hungry. (He feeds the animals.)
He's eating, he's eating OK.
You gotta be nice. I'll hit him.
Go rob the bank, lizard!

(*A girl arrives at the house door.*)

Boy: Mrs. Duke said no one can come in here.
Girl (moving in anyway): But I'm the doctor.
Boys: No, no one can come in. This is the animal store. We live here.

(*Three more girls arrive. One of the boys, clearly feeling overwhelmed, points a gun made of Unifix cubes.*)

"We police," he announces.
Another boy: There's too much girls in here.

Mrs. Duke decides it's time for arbitration rather than shooting. "No guns, DeShaun," she says. "We need to keep it safe for the animals."

She negotiates the girls into the adjacent floor-block area, which has its own supply of animals. "We're playing zoo again," a girl announces. (Reynolds & Jones, 1997, pp. 86–87)

Mrs. Duke has succeeded in defining space to permit parallel/cooperative play, which flows back and forth for the next half hour, as a zoo is built by both girls and boys and the pet store offers resources to the zoo-keepers. These 4- and 5-year-olds are master imaginers, and so is their child-care teacher.

INVENTING: THE PLAY ENVIRONMENT

Symbolic play is learned through imitation and imagination. If Mommy, or Daddy, cooks a lot, young children start cooking too. But Mommy and Daddy don't cook sand or autumn leaves or toy snakes, and sometimes children do. Parents don't usually play monster, except on very bad days or perhaps at a Halloween party. But many children do, because there are monsters in stories, monsters on video, and monsters in their very own nightmares.

Children get play ideas from all their experiences and from their friends' experiences. Children fortunate enough to spend time in mixed-age groups get ideas from older children. And they get ideas from playful adults.

The five children, ages 5 to 15, all clamored to sit in front by their father at the beginning of a drive to the country. The older boys resigned them-selves when their sister was given the privileged place, but the 5-year-old twins howled in shared rage.

"Stop that noise at once!" shouted their father, unheard above the din.

Their grandmother, who was seeing them off, understood her grandchil-dren better than anyone.

"In royal procession," she told them, "the king and queen always sit in the back of the car with outriders to either side . . ."

The twins' yells ceased as though a tap had been turned off, and in no time at all the family had settled themselves in the car in the positions she had indicated. The twins bowed to right and left with shattering dignity. (adapted from Goudge, 1948, pp. 77–79)

INVESTIGATING: THE SCHOOL ENVIRONMENT

Do older children get to play in school? If not, they lose important opportunities for "breathing out"—representing in their own ways the skills and ideas they're being taught. Recess isn't enough, in its common 20-minute version in crowded space with few playthings. Serious play takes longer than that.

Do teachers get to play in school? If not, they lose opportunities for the sort of interactive learning that lets them know what their children really understand. Denied permission to deviate from prescribed curriculum, they lose the mental stimulation of on-the-spot decision making. They lose, too, the joy of play and its role in building relationships and shared pleasure. "Sometimes," my (Betty) daughter's first-grade teacher once told me, "I get to laughing with the children and it's really fun. But then we have to stop it and get back to work." Not surprisingly, my daughter remembers her with fondness.

An adult colleague commented recently, "The teachers I still remember were either creative or playful." Lasting memories are based in relationships.

A Classroom Where Play Is Not OK

In this 3-hour afternoon kindergarten class, most activities during the first 2 hours are sedentary; children sit at tables or in a circle on the rug. Then there's a 20-minute outdoor recess. Today it's followed by journal writing at 2:25 P.M., group sharing on the rug at 2:40 P.M. At 2:47 P.M. the teacher puts on an action-song record and invites the children to stand up and follow the movements in the song. They are delighted and exuberant. She abruptly turns off the record.

"Those are NOT the motions of our song. No jumping. No hopping. One two three four." The record is turned back on and the children are subdued, carefully doing it right but without joy. Only hand motions are allowed; the feet are supposed to stay still.

Why? What's wrong with hopping and jumping? What is the teacher afraid of?

Balance is the issue in providing for playful learning at school—a balance between *breathing in* and *breathing out* (Ashton-Warner, 1963). In this kindergarten there isn't much balance between sitting and moving. There isn't much balance between convergent and divergent thinking.

Some aspects of balance change as children grow older. Young toddlers need to move until they drop; controlling their muscles is the most important thing they're learning. Eight-year-olds, most of them, can sit still for quite a while—though many of the control issues in primary classrooms result from the behavior of little boys (mostly) who need to *move*. *Industry*—learning to work at focused tasks—is the developmental challenge for children in school. But the need for balance between convergent and divergent thinking doesn't go away. A convergent task tells you: This is how you do it. Practice doing it right. A divergent task invites you: What are all the ways someone could do this?

In a movement activity like that described above, playful teachers leave room for innovations like hopping and jumping. They may even encourage them: "Oh, you thought of jumping. How high can you jump? Can you jump without bumping Rasheel?" "You're jumping on one foot, aren't you? That's hopping." "The person on the record had some ideas for what to do with this music. And you had some other ideas, too. Good for you!"

A Classroom Where Play Is OK

Fewer teachers, perhaps, adopt a playful, divergent approach to spelling and handwriting. Here's a particularly imaginative one, following an alphabet lesson that began, "This is an *A*. Let's all practice writing it. Watch how I do it. I go up like this, and down like this, and across like this. *A*!"

And then:

Who has an *A* in their name? Yes, Alicia, you do. And you could write it like this: ALICIA. Or like this: Alicia. Or like this: *Alicia*—but maybe you won't do that until second grade. That's pretty tricky, isn't it—to have so many ways to write a name?

One thing you can do with your name is to write it on your drawing, so we'll know whose it is when it's time to go home. Let's think about that. If you don't want your drawing to get lost, what are all the ways you could label it so everybody will know whose it is?

When you were 3 years old and didn't know how to write yet, what did you do? Right, I bet a grownup wrote it for you.

Suppose you were 4 and you had just learned to write an *A*, but not any other letters. What could you do? Yep, you could just write the *A*. *A* for *Alicia*. Then would everybody know?

Nope, says Alex. It might be mine!

Then maybe Alicia would need to write *A G* for *Alicia Gutierrez*. Alex, do you know what letter your last name begins with?

Conversations of this sort elicit more child talk than teacher talk, as children get intrigued and think of more ideas. (It's children, not teachers, who need practice talking in school.)

Do you know, says the teacher, that some kids write their names backward? Like this: AIƆIⱯ.

Hey, says Alex, she's got an *A* on both ends!

She does, doesn't she? the teacher agrees. Whichever way she writes it, it's still got an *A* on both ends. But yours doesn't. If we did yours backward it would be ⱯƎⱢⱯ.

Clearly, this is not a single day's discussion in a class of 5- or 6-year-olds. It's part of a whole year's discussion of all the ways in which English—and other languages—is tricky, demanding lots of paying attention and good thinking by children whose heads are full of ideas. All along, it reinforces the basic handwriting lesson: This is an *A*, and these are the many, many ways to remember it and use it. And then children-being-helpers can take responsibility for sorting the drawings to send home at the end of the day, using all the clues they've talked about, and chastising kids who forgot to put their name or whatever on their papers. In a classroom community you're not accountable just to your teacher for the quality of your work. Writing is communication to everybody.

There is no guaranteed memory strategy. In any group of children there will be visual learners, auditory learners, kinesthetic learners (can you make an *A* with your bodies?), and learners who need a joke in order to embed an idea in their heads. Good teachers use them all and engage in play for themselves as they go along. (How, this teacher is trying to remember, do you write *Alicia* in Greek? Greek being an alphabet she learned just for fun while driving past fraternity houses in college. There was that cool guy in Sigma Chi . . . Σ X.)

PLAY IN THE STAGE OF GENERATIVITY: TEACHERS AT PLAY

Consider the changes in taste that aging brings:

As the well-preserved princess walks along the side of the pond, a frog suddenly appears.

"Kiss me!" begs the frog. "Kiss me and I will turn into a handsome prince."

The princess laughs. "At this point in my life I'm more interested in a talking frog."

Teaching without joy is a deadening experience for both teachers and children. We go through the motions. We learn, and we forget.

How can we help adults—teachers and parents—find joy in spending their days with children? We're advocates for complicating the task by inviting them to pay attention to the details of children's discoveries. Both of us, Renatta and Betty, as teacher educators, parent educators, and teachers of young children, are kid watchers first and foremost, endlessly fascinated by what we see and continually alert to ways to turn others on to what we see.

There may be, it is true, other sources of satisfaction in caregiving and teaching. For example, for those born homemakers whose delight is in creating and sustaining beautiful order in living spaces (and who view messes as a welcome challenge), caring for babies may be particularly satisfying, since babies aren't expected to help with cleanup and thus battles of wills don't arise. In contrast, there are born coaches whose joy comes in challenging children to practice skills and become more and more competent, at sports, playing an instrument, even handwriting. Children's performance—in a recital, on the playing field, on tests—gives visible evidence of their success and ours. These are the moments at which the much overused words "Good job!" become really meaningful.

Why did the seal get average grades?
He was really a C lion.

But preschool teachers always used to say (do they still?) that it's the process, not the product, that matters in early childhood. For many of us who gravitated to early childhood education, our joy is in the process: the drama, humor, and unexpectednesses out of which stories are made. I (Betty) used to say, with truth, that my real reasons for having a lot of children were that I love reading children's books and was in need of a captive audience, and that I was also endlessly curious about who the next child would turn out to be.

Some folks working with young children, however, got there by default; they aren't college qualified to be "real" teachers but wish they were. Can we entice more of them, whoever they are, to believe in play? To support play?

Telling Teachers Their Stories

Working in an urban school district in a 5-year staff-development project, I (Betty) observed regularly in classrooms, collecting stories about children's play and language to be shared in a weekly newsletter. My intent was to support teachers' growth

by observing children in their classrooms, scribing observations in words and pictures, and engaging in conversations in which teachers' and observer's perceptions are shared. In these interactions teachers experience a process equally appropriate for their interactions with children. (Jones, 1993, p. xx)

Who tells teachers their stories? As human beings we are affirmed in our competence and self-understanding by others' retelling of their experiences with us. Teaching is a very daily and, often, isolating task. While the adult world goes on about its business outside the classroom, the teacher of young children is in constant contact with immature minds. These minds are stimulating in their own right, to be sure, and worthy of the best that caring adults can give them, but they are not the teacher's peers. To sustain both enthusiasm and critical thinking about their work, teachers need response from professional peers offering both affirmation and intellectual challenge.

Teachers Telling Their Own Stories

One of the first discussions I (Renatta) had with the students in my recent community college class was on the importance of play in the learning process. My remarks were greeted with varying degrees of skepticism. Many adults, especially those from low-income groups under pressure to have their children succeed in school, are more convinced by flash cards and drill than by play. "What did you learn at school today?" A child who has memorized facts is often eager to show them off; that's reassuring. "We just played" isn't. But if I cannot convince this group of early childhood educators about the validity of play, I am not a very effective advocate.

My first assignment for them was to write a one-to-two-page essay on the role of play in their own learning process. "What if you haven't learned anything through play?" asked Gloria, a retired African-American woman who would like to work with young children after a career with seniors. "You have," I assured her. "You all have. It may take you some time to think about it, because much of what you learned through play you now take for granted."

The assignment elicited some very interesting responses:

When I was about 6 years old I would go into our backyard and make plates and bowls out of mud. I loved pretending that what I made would be used to eat on. I would mix the dirt with different things to see what made it harden as a plate and still keep its form. Grass worked best. When I left my creations out in the sun, sometimes they would dry into recognizable bowls and plates, and sometimes not. However, the finished product did not really matter to me that much.

It was unusual for me to enjoy an activity that resulted in getting dirty. And this was something I did by myself, not with my big sister. I think this is where I began to explore creativity, where I learned about how ingredients change the product.—Antoinette

My mother and father were very involved in the church in our community; therefore the church was built into our creative play. Usually I was the one to plan the Sunday-morning service. I always selected my younger brother to be the preacher because he liked dressing in a shirt and tie and sometimes a robe and pretending that he was preaching. I would organize the pulpit, then I would select choir members, next I would set up chairs for the congregation, and then each of us would role-play what we had learned from church on Sunday.

This play made me feel important, worthwhile, and successful as a human being.—Mildred

I learned about cooking while playing in my play kitchen in the clubhouse in my backyard, and driving by playing behind the wheel of my bicycle. I learned caring for babies while playing with my dolls, and drawing because of the many doodles I wrote throughout my school days. But more importantly, I learned management skills by using my imagination on a regular basis. I would play with superheroes in my living room: conducting meetings, giving assignments, matching partners for crime-stopping situations, and keeping the peace, between high-profile assignments and subsequent recognition.—Dorian

Some culture-specific images also emerged from this assignment. Among the many who "played school," I noted that where African Americans typically indicated, "I was always the teacher," the Latinas typically wrote, "Sometimes I was the teacher." Is this a reflection of personality, recall, or a more collaborative culture?

My friends loved my game because I always gave them 100% as a grade. Some of them had lower grades at school. The classes I had at school inspired me to develop my game; for instance, we sang the ABC, and I repeated some phrases my teacher said to students in class. I used to say "Sonia, give me your homework," and when Sonia answered, "I didn't do it," I said, "Bring it tomorrow, OK?"—Linda

Supporting Play: Experiencing a Play Environment

Renatta's assignment asked students to practice the believing game by reflecting on childhood memories. If you are a teacher of adults, as we are, we urge you to insist that your students play in your classes, with ideas and memories and one another. College teachers, just like teachers of children, often get anxious about "covering all the material," a worry that frequently translates into teaching to the test. But testable "facts" are superficial. Your clever students will outfox you by memorizing your words and feeding them back to you on the test, and then go right on teaching children the way they always have.

Workshops, trainings, and college classes for early childhood educators become most memorable if they are structured as *play environments*, adapting the strategies of an early childhood classroom to provide a model as well as a "developmentally appropriate" active learning experience for adults (Jones, 1986). To be a play leader for children, one must master play for oneself. Adults are capable players with words, with materials, and with their bodies; adult education should foster the disposition to play with possibilities rather than follow a learned script. Questions that don't have a right answer, that encourage divergent thinking and story sharing, are the most powerful in encouraging adults to construct knowledge for themselves. Knowledge not owned by the knower is unlikely to find its way into her work site.

Play with Words

Words are useful for telling personal stories, sharing observations of children, playing with ideas (connecting one's own named experiences with other people's organized naming, that is, theories), and as playthings in their own right (poetry, jokes, song lyrics, word games) to be tossed around and made into patterns. Renatta's questions to her class: How did you play as a child? What did you learn by playing? insisted that they move past skepticism to the power of personal stories.

Adults need to play with memories like these and share them with one another. ("Really? Did you do that? So did I, but mine . . ."). In reflecting on experience, they are constructing knowledge that is applicable to their professional work. In reconnecting with strong feelings, they have an opportunity to reexamine some of the reasons why they may do what they do now.

For example, many adults who teach children seem to have an overwhelming need to "play school." "School" is a game often played by kids in ritual fashion, with the Mean Teacher in charge. Like many of the other games of childhood, it features good guys and bad guys. Like all dramatic play, it offers the chance to switch and to redefine roles. Thus Linda, quoted above, could be an especially nice teacher, giving everyone 100% (even though real teachers don't do that). She acknowledged her transformative approach: "I enjoyed the school game because the teacher was always happy. And the students could make suggestions about the class, or complain if they felt the teacher wasn't correct."

Adults sharing memories can role-play them as well as talk about them. In a class Betty taught, where small groups were asked to create role plays to practice and then present to the group, the most memorable play featured a formidable Sister Mary Catherine, ruler in hand, terrorizing the rest. The follow-up discussion brought out many memories of fear and conformity, and pleasurable relief at the opportunity to play these out as adults.

Adults need to play with ideas, and here's where instructor scaffolding comes in:

Let's look at the stories you've been telling us about your childhood play. Some of you said, when I gave you that assignment, that you didn't learn anything by playing. Did some of you change your minds? Do some of you still hold that view? Be courageous; tell us what you think.

We're inventing our theory about the uses of play in childhood. Let's make some lists:

What do children learn by playing?
What *don't* they learn by playing? What things have
to be learned in other ways?

The image of real learning as Teacher in Front of Group, Talking, is burned into all our brains. Is that what goes on in your college classroom? It doesn't have to. If you're talking more than your students are, relook at the possibilities; try "teaching with your mouth shut" (Finkel, 2000). Instructor lectures can be minilectures, short presentations to launch small-group discussions. Other lectures emerge out of large-group discussion, as someone makes a point that the instructor wants to enlarge upon.

Student presenters also need to use their imaginations; in classes with individual student reports on projects, just listening can get pretty old. A creative alternative is task-group presentations for which the instructions are, You will have 15 minutes to let us know something about what you did and learned. Your presentation must (a) involve all of you, (b) involve all of us, and (c) be nonverbal as well as verbal.

Play with Materials

Adults need to play with some of the open-ended materials used by children—blocks, especially, and perhaps play dough and wet sand. They need to talk about their discoveries:

What does this do?
What can I do with it?

What can a 3-year-old do with it?
How can it be made inviting to children?
What is a child learning while playing with this?

I (Betty) have led hands-on workshops for early childhood teachers featuring blocks and play dough and inviting the participants to choose from among closed, partially open, and open-ended activities. Homemade play dough, for example, was available in several different colors. Each table offered a different task:

1. Use the green play dough to make seven worms and five rocks. Put one worm under each rock. How many worms are left over? Put the leftover worms back in the dough container.
2. Use all three colors of play dough to make balls of different sizes. Can you put spots on any of the balls? Stripes?
3. What would you like to make with all this play dough? You can talk to your friends about what you might do together, or work by yourself.

Predictably, it was often hard to get the third group to stop playing when it was time for debriefing: What did you learn about play dough? Yourself? Children?

Play with Bodies

Adults need to play some active, silly games with one another, in order to loosen up their thinking and their bodies, to share their fears. Remember *El Lobo* in Chapter 5? Here's Catch:

Stand in a circle. I'm going to throw this bean bag to one of you. You throw it to someone else, and so on. When everyone has gotten it, throw it back to me. *Remember the pattern*—who threw it to you, whom you threw it to.

OK, it's back to me. Let's do it again. Remember the pattern.

I'm starting again. Whatever happens, remember the pattern. (And soon after the bean bag is making its rounds again, I pull a stuffed monkey out of the big bag at my feet and throw that, still in the pattern. There are gasps of surprise. That goes on for a bit, and then I produce another object, and another, and another—a stuffed frog, a small pillow, a sock stuffed with another sock, a ball, a plastic measuring cup, a stuffed turtle, a short string of big plastic beads, a soft slipper—maybe more. When chaos reigns, I stop.)

Toss everything back into the middle of the circle. What kind of experience was that for you? How did you feel? Did you learn anything?

Physically active play makes new kinds of connections in a group of learners. For a few, it brings up fears. ("I can't stand having things coming at me"; "I got really scared when you kept saying, 'Don't forget the pattern.' It felt like a test or something.") For some, it's pure fun and laughter. For some, those who have trouble sitting still for long, it's a physical release. Do children have all these different experiences, too, when we have them play organized games, and even when they're inventing their own play? Food for thought.

SUMMING UP: THE POWER OF BEING AN AUTHOR

We think this is how development happens, how learning works, and how the world should work, and we have just spent the last hundred or so pages telling you all about it. We trust that those of you who believed us when you started the book have enjoyed having your views confirmed. We have asked the rest of you to practice the believing game as you read, looking for experiences of your own that confirm the truth of our words. That's pretty arrogant of us—but then, being an author is a pretty heady experience. Back in Chapter 1 we quoted JoeAnn Dugger's words to her class of adults: Everybody has a theory. Some people write theirs down and become famous. We're not seeking fame, exactly, but we'd like you to agree with us.

That's not fair, unless we also acknowledge your point of view and play the believing game in turn. Are we entitled to the last word? Not without the discipline of renewed practice in taking the view of the other. We invite you to join us in the Epilogue—after one more joke.

> When Rudolf wakes up, he looks out of the tent, and a drop falls on his auburn head.
> "It's raining," he says.
> "No, it can't rain today," insists his little girl.
> "But it is," he assures her. "I'm Rudolf the Red, right?"
> "Right," she agrees.
> "Well, Rudolf the Red knows rain, dear."

Epilogue:
What's Wrong
with This Picture?

Cave canem: Beware of the dog.
Caveat emptor: Let the buyer beware.
Caveat magistra: Let the teacher beware. (This one may be wrong.
    Betty's high school Latin is a bit rusty.)

IN fact, it's possible that we've been wrong all the way through this book. We don't think so, but we may not have convinced you. If not, this afterword is for you. In it, we want to do two things:

1. Acknowledge the limitations of our view of things, as presented in the last hundred pages.
2. Take a turn at playing the believing game ourselves, to remind us of how hard it is.

RESISTING CHANGE

William Penn, the founder of Pennsylvania, was a follower of the Quaker faith. But he was also a soldier, and Quakers are pacifists. He wrestled with this contradiction in his daily meditations, and one day Quaker leader George Fox, Penn's mentor, said to him, "William, thee must wear thy sword as long as thee can."

The moral of this story is: Don't change your behavior or belief until you can do no other. Transformative learning—shifting one's perspective—is not to be undertaken lightly; it requires too much energy for too long. If your basic assumptions guide you well, don't question them. It's only when discrepancies creep in, when you begin to feel that your behavior doesn't match your values, that it's time to reexamine your personal theory and practice.

Pat Adams (2003), a former preschool teacher now a college instructor, has written about her transformation from resister of developmentally appropriate curriculum, to strong advocate. She's been a resister all her life, she explains. As a child in home and neighborhood, she was free to play, but school was something else again, in a class of 50 children where obedience was the priority. Dyslexic, she didn't do well. By middle school, her self-defined goal was to be Bad. As a young adult, she headed for the north woods to become a "timber beast."

Later, with children of her own, she found a job in child care. She was horrified by its developmental approach, and she completely disagreed with the philosophy of the early childhood education classes she was required to take to keep her job. In her classes, she memorized for the tests. At work, having failed to shape everybody up to the authoritarian standards she had learned in her own schooling, she found another child-care center that shared them. Only after settling in there did she start paying attention to children as individuals, gradually becoming a playful teacher.

When she became a college instructor she taught developmentally appropriate practice—and wondered why her students didn't follow through with it on the job. She has since decided that play is important for adult learners too, and challenges them to practice risk taking (risk taking is a skill they really need, she says) on a climbing wall, among other places.

As you might guess, we authors have our own histories of resistance. Developmentally appropriate practice was a shoo-in for me (Betty) long before that's what it was called. When I first walked into a preschool (as a graduate student), I didn't intend to become a teacher; my interest was observing children at play. It still is. My challenges came as a teacher of adults, memorably provoked by a colleague (Bill Baker) who asked me, in genuine curiosity: How come you give choices to children but not to adults? I denied it, thought about it, and spent the next dozen years of my teaching figuring out how to structure classes for adults according to the constructivist principles I used with children (Jones, 1986).

Much later, I found myself faced with another level of challenge: How to structure online classes to be as interactive as those I had invented for face-to-face instruction. Here the challenge was letting go of my determination never to use a computer. (My mother chose never to drive a car or buy an automatic washing machine; I had good role modeling.) I am still suspicious of computers, but I love e-mail.

As a graduate student I (Renatta) was enrolled in a program for parent educators. I was the only person of color and was younger than most of the other students. They were parents and sometimes grandparents; I was neither. They saw themselves as parenting experts, especially with families who were comfortably off.

My experience was with lower-income parents, and my style of working with them was to share power, not play expert. My instructor was worried, when I didn't say much in discussions, that I was feeling alienated. But I didn't expect to be comfortable; I just wasn't about to argue with these folks. I wrote a lot in my class journal, arguing against the idea that I would be that expert.

It's 30 years later, and next week I'm giving a workshop on parenting Black babies. I'll be inside my own culture, and I'm the sage in that presentation. I'm graying, I'm experienced, I'm comfortable in the role of elder—of expert.

I'm comfortable as expert with White parents too. I know a lot about them and their goals, and I can support them in those goals that I feel are not oppressive to me or to others like me.

Having enjoyed and thrived on resistance ourselves, we honor other resisters—at least in principle, if not always in person when they're resisting us. We owe it to our readers, then, to be as honest as we can about the possible pitfalls of the principles we advocate in this book. Sometimes they may not work in the real world, for any of the reasons that follow.

LET THE READER BEWARE: ACKNOWLEDGING OUR LIMITATIONS

Caveat: The Importance of Being Fierce

One upon a time when I (Betty) was juggling a large family of growing kids and teaching college classes in early childhood education and advocating for all the sorts of stuff I'm still advocating for in this book, my friend and colleague Liz Prescott complained to me that I was misrepresenting my approach to parenting and teaching young children. "You don't tell them how fierce a parent you are," she said. "None of it would work without that." She was right, and still is.

I (Renatta) am even fiercer than Betty. Vernon (in Chapter 6) knew that when he went inside with me even though I didn't chase him.

A baby's first developmental task is to learn *trust*. Human babies are extraordinarily vulnerable; there is practically nothing they can do for themselves. Baby alligators go hunting. Baby geese can eat grass. Baby monkeys cling firmly to their mama's fur as she swings through the trees. Even half-finished baby kangaroos can crawl up their mama's pouch wall and attach themselves firmly to the teat. Baby people just lie there and howl. They need intensive care, often exhausting their parents.

The first level of care is food, the second is warmth, the next is cleaning. Much of the rest is about safety (not falling off things, and so on). Premobile babies, who don't need fierce protection from their own behavior (only from those alligators and other predators), quickly grow into creepers, crawlers, and toddlers determined to master their territory at all costs. Their first word is "No!"—understandably, since that's the first important command they encounter in their young lives. However dressed up with reasons (often at the expense of clarity, in some households), a fierce "No!" is the basic word for keeping a toddler safe.

Are we contradicting most of the rest of this book? Yes, indeed. As they grow past infancy, children need many, many opportunities to get smart—to think, to reason, to argue, to experience the consequences of disobedience. But the first responsibility of adults is to provide safe boundaries within which to do these wonderful things. To be appropriately fierce.

Caveat: The Importance of Regression

For a teacher otherwise inclined toward power WITH, fierceness with children is *regression* to a less demanding set of behaviors. We all get tired. We can't be at our best all the time. Play, emergent curriculum, and democracy are a lot more work than prescribed order. They are inherently more work, requiring thinking on one's feet, endless decision making, and collaboration with others who are not like us.

Mike, as a 1st-year teacher, was eager to provide explorations in science for his third graders. One afternoon, with lots of choices of activities, things got pretty well out of hand. The kids were yelling happily as the balloons sailed around, and soon Mike was yelling in frustration. The kids subsided, and when everything was put away, he said to the class: "We've been trying democracy in this class, and it isn't working. So next week we'll be trying dictatorship. I'm the dictator. You can decide which you like better, and at the end of the week we'll vote."

Gloria, an experienced first-grade teacher, had been doing basal reading groups for some years when she was asked to try a more complex, individualized approach to reading and writing. She did, cooperating with other teachers in a lively team effort. But the next year she went back to the basals.

"Didn't it work?" a teacher friend asked her.

"It was great for the kids," said Gloria. "But it was a lot more work for me. When it comes down to a choice between time with my family and time spent preparing for teaching, it's no contest. The basals are OK, and I can do them with very little thought. And the principal approves of my nice quiet classroom."

Divergent approaches are not only more work, they carry more risk. In settings where authority is valued, teachers who ease up on control risk getting in trouble. At another time Gloria's principal said to a consultant who had questioned the quality of learning in one of the classes in his school (where children did worksheets constantly and there was no talking), "Yes, but she's really got them under control. That other teacher may have good ideas, as you claim, but control comes first."

This view is easy to sell to parents and public, even to teachers. Constance Kamii, describing her own basic change of philosophy from behaviorism to constructivism, writes about *common sense* as the precursor to both these scientific theories. "According to common sense, teaching consists of *telling* or *presenting* knowledge, and learning takes place by the *internalization* of what is taught" (1985, p. 4). What could be simpler? Kamii refuses to accept this simplicity. "Worksheets are harmful for first graders' development of arithmetic," she states flatly, "while play is highly beneficial." Number concepts are not teachable. However, "we don't have to teach number concepts because children will construct them on their own" (p. 6).

Education is an amazing profession in which professionals can be forced to do things against their conscience. Physicians are not forced to give treatments that only make the symptoms disappear, but many teachers give phonics lessons and worksheets, knowing perfectly well that the imposition of the 3 R's may make children dislike school and lose confidence in their own ability to figure things out. (p. 3)

Constructivists emphasize the importance of learning to write by discovering that "my words make print" and gradually inventing for oneself, with support, all the technical components of written language. That's a more challenging task for both children and teachers than Pamela's simply writing sentences on the board for her second graders to copy. "In the afternoon they're too tired to do their own thinking," she explained. Maybe she was, too, and so regression was the order of the day.

Caveat: The Importance of Order—Keeping Things Tidy

Safety, and adult fear of kids en masse, aren't the only reasons we set boundaries for children—and ourselves. Tidiness is a virtue in its own right; it helps us live with one another and find the things we need.

Many things have to be done exactly right. Telephoning and e-mail are among our daily examples—get one number or letter wrong and you won't connect. Dirt or spilled coffee jams computers. Running a stop light can get you killed. Slovenly bottom-wiping leads to diaper rash. If your violin's A is just a mite flat, every musical ear in the audience will wince. Being careful and accurate is very, very important in many aspects of our lives.

We don't invent tidiness; we're instructed in it, reminded, nagged, punished. We imitate the desirable behavior of our adult models. (However, nearly all adults retain pockets of resistance: clothes on the floor, dirty dishes in the sink, top off the toothpaste tube.)

Many physical skills, from golf to saxophone, are learned through coaching—imitate, correct, and try, try again. There are known ways to do these things right; if you want the gold medal, you have to work for it without argument.

Caveat for the Other Side

(Yes, we've just evaded this chapter's rules. So much for playing fair. Writers have power.)

Our argument on behalf of order, above, is only half the picture (and we can't resist telling you so). Being accurate isn't the equivalent of being smart, even though spelling tests try to create that impression. Really smart means being able to think outside the box when right turns out to be wrong. Advising new online learners, Judy Magee has written about computers: "Stuff going wrong is normal and manageable. . . . There's nearly always a way to work around a problem. When the front door to a feature doesn't work, you can often crawl through a back door or window" (Magee & Jones, 2004, p. 15).

To survive online with one's sanity, "exactly right" needs to become a game to be played, not the Rules of the World. "Aha, little e-mail address, I'll get you right this time" is the most fruitful response to a kicked-back error message. It's like inventive spelling; *thinking* really helps one cope with mistakes. And we're back to What are all the ways you could spell *nite*? Come to think of it, it's a lot like teaching little children, ingenious creatures that they are. Just as we've got it right, they make us wrong again.

Caveat: The Importance of Doing Things
Even if They're Boring

It is not possible ever to create a learning environment or work environment or home environment that is always interesting. Just being in a group requires adaptation, patience, and learning the survival skills of sneaking and not getting in trouble. Small solutions include doodling, daydreaming, knitting, and deftly passing notes to one's neighbor—harmless games to pass the time. Children can also be taught to hang in there by the promise of a reward; and in some classrooms, the reward is play time.

"You've worked so well this morning," said Juan with a smile at his first graders. "I think it's time to get out the toys." Clearly, this was a practiced routine: Jump ropes, dolls, My Little Ponies, and even a small trampoline appeared as if by magic (the children knew just where to get them and put them), and children negotiated skillfully among the desks for 20 minutes of well-earned action. In another first grade in another town, Rosi schedules a regular PAT (Preferred Activity Time—if it's got an acronym it must be educational!), which can, however, be forfeited if children fail to get through the routines efficiently that day.

Groups of children impatient with civilized responses to boredom often introduce the game of Uproar. This delightful game is played for the sheer drama of it, partly out of boredom, partly out of anger at the adults in their world, and partly out of real curiosity: If we make her mad, what will she do? Are there boundaries, and where are they? Will she keep things safe if they get out of hand? Teachers need to learn to recognize this game when they see it, and either nip it in the bud or elaborate it to one-up the kids. The Importance of Being Fierce is especially relevant when kids are engaged in testing limits. *Because I said so and I'm the grownup* is, after all, the ultimate good reason. Children need us to take care of them.

WE PRACTICE THE BELIEVING GAME

At the beginning of this chapter, we promised to take a turn at playing the believing game ourselves, in order to remember how hard it is. To remind you of the rules, this game asks us not for naive credulity, but for a conscious effort to understand why someone might believe what we don't. "In what senses or under what conditions," Peter Elbow asks, "might this idea be true?" (1986, p. 275).

Elbow values doubt, describing it as "the human struggle to free ourselves from parochial closed mindedness." But he adds,

It doesn't go far enough. Methodological doubt caters too comfortably to our natural impulse to protect and retain the views we already hold. Methodological belief comes to the rescue at this point by forcing us genuinely to enter into unfamiliar or threatening ideas instead of just arguing against them without experiencing them or feeling their force. It thus carries us *further* on in our developmental journey away from mere credulity. (p. 263)

He challenges his readers to play the believing game. ·

"I respect faith, but doubt is what gets you an education" (Cross, 1990, p. 166).

Both of us are temperamentally inclined toward doubt, not belief, when things get hairy. We enjoy critical thinking as play and encourage our students, little and big, to engage in it too. But I (Renatta) was reared in a faith-based community; my (Betty's) parents were; and we have many friends and colleagues whose faith is central to their lives. Our practicing empathy, then, is eased by its personal connections; it's easier to doubt one's enemies than one's friends.

Why is devotion to revealed truth a good thing? If we move from doubt to the believing game, we can quite easily recognize the following:

Received knowledge frees one to do one's work without complaining, without wasting energy in resistance: "The Lord is my shepherd; I shall not want. He leadeth me in the paths of righteousness for his name's sake. Surely goodness and mercy shall follow me all the days of my life and I shall dwell in the house of the Lord forever."

If I follow the faith and tradition of my family and community, I am assured of love.

Basic trust is a virtue. Interdependence holds the community together—and keeps me safe.

That wasn't hard; let's take it a step further. We have organized this book around some of our most cherished assumptions. Are we brave enough to turn them on their heads and argue on behalf of their opposites? Here we go.

Assumption: Complexity is more interesting than simplicity.
Revised Assumption: As any good preschool teacher knows, children get confused in an overstimulating environment. Think of the beautiful order in a Montessori classroom.

Assumption: Intrinsic motivation is more efficient than relying on rewards and punishments.
Revised Assumption: Extrinsic motivation is necessary. Children are not yet like us; we need to shape their behavior into what's right, and so rewards and punishments (also called threats and bribes) are necessary as well as modeling. You can't just let them do what they want to. Efficient? That's ridiculous. As members of a group,

individuals can't get special attention, and it wouldn't be good for their characters, anyway. (Betty recognized, as her children went off to their neighborhood public school, that this is what they would learn there, and that would be good for them, as an instructive contrast with home.)

Assumption: Democracy is a better bet than dictatorship. Sharing power is safer than trying to hang on to it all. To liberate is wiser, in the long run, than to domesticate.

Revised Assumption: Democracy has to be earned. You can't give children freedom before they've learned responsibility. Of course they have to be domesticated, just like other small animals. You let kids get away with things, they'll take advantage of you.

Assumption: Becoming consciously bicultural is more powerful than either assimilating or maintaining separateness.

Revised Assumption: This is an English-speaking country. Those foreigners expect to live here, they've got to learn our ways. The sooner the better for them and for us, *or*

Train up your children in the way they should go, and they will not depart therefrom. Children need a guarded education, within their own cultural community; they need to be protected from those other people who don't act right.

So, we have given you more than half of our assumptions, deconstructed. We invite you to add to these and to take on the rest. If you must.

There is more than one way to accomplish just about anything. Real life, beyond the wordplay of writing and reading a book, is a question of finding a balance.

Save the Earth. It's the only planet with chocolate.

References

Adams, P. (2003). *Stories and reflections on emerging into a child centered philosophy: Teaching, learning, and change.* Unpublished master's thesis, Pasadena, CA: Pacific Oaks College.

Ashton-Warner, S. (1963). *Teacher.* New York: Simon & Schuster.

Belenky, M. F., Clinchy, B. M., Goldberger, N. R., & Tarule, J. M. (1986). *Women's ways of knowing: The development of self, voice, and mind.* New York: Basic Books.

Bissex, G. (1980). *GNYS at work: A child learns to write and read.* Cambridge: Harvard University Press.

Bruno, H. E. (2003). Hearing parents in every language: An invitation to ECE professionals. *Child Care Information Exchange, 153,* 58–60.

Carlsson-Paige, N., & Levin, D. (1987). *The war play dilemma: Balancing needs and values in the early childhood classroom.* New York: Teachers College Press.

Carney, L. C. (1978). *Redefining the teacher's role as authority: A theoretical approach for the open classroom* (Occasional Paper). Pacific Oaks College, Pasadena, CA.

Carroll, L. (1979). *Alice in Wonderland and Through the looking glass.* New York: Grosset & Dunlap.

Coles, R. (1989). *The call of stories: Teaching and the moral imagination.* Boston: Houghton Mifflin.

Cooper, R. M. (1996). The role of play in the acculturation process. In A. L. Phillips (Ed.), *Playing for keeps: Supporting children's play* (pp. 89–98). St. Paul, MN: Redleaf.

Cooper, R. M. (1999). "But they're only playing": Interpreting play to parents. *Child Care Information Exchange, 125,* 55–57.

Creech, S. (2000). *The wanderer.* New York: HarperCollins.

Cronin, S., & Sosa Massó, C. (2003). *Soy bilingüe: Language, culture, and young Latino children.* Seattle: Center for Linguistic and Cultural Democracy.

Cross, A. (1990). *The players come again.* London: Virago.

Csikszentmihalyi, M. (1975). *Beyond boredom and anxiety.* San Francisco: Jossey-Bass.

Cummins, J. (1986). Empowering minority students: A framework for intervention. *Harvard Educational Review, 56*(1), 18–36.

Delpit, L. (1995). *Other people's children: Cultural conflict in the classroom.* New York: New Press.

Dewey, J. (1940). The need for a philosophy of education. In *Education today,* (pp. 288–299). New York: Putnam. (Original work published 1934)

Dewey, J. (1964). My pedagogic creed. In R. Archambault (Ed.), *John Dewey on Education: Selected writings*. Chicago: University of Chicago Press.

Dewey, J. (1966). *Democracy and education*. New York: Free Press. (Original work published 1916)

Donaldson, M. (1978). *Children's minds*. New York: Norton.

Dyson, A. H. (2003). *The brothers and sisters learn to write: Popular literacies in childhood and school cultures*. New York: Teachers College Press.

Egan, K. (1986). *Teaching as storytelling: An alternative approach to teaching and curriculum in the elementary school*. Chicago: University of Chicago Press.

Eisner, E. (2002). *The arts and the creation of mind*. New Haven: Yale University Press.

Eisner, E. (2005, January 3). Three Rs are essential but don't forget the A. *Los Angeles Times*, p. B15.

Elbow, P. (1986). *Embracing contraries: Explorations in teaching and learning*. New York: Oxford University Press.

Erikson, E. H. (1950). *Childhood and society*. New York: Norton.

Finkel, D. L. (2000). *Teaching with your mouth shut*. Portsmouth, NH: Boynton/Cook.

Freire, P. (1970). *Pedagogy of the oppressed*. New York: Seabury.

Gallas, K. (1995). *Talking their way into science: Hearing children's questions and theories, responding with curricula*. New York: Teachers College Press.

Gallas, K. (1998). *"Sometimes I can be anything": Power and gender identity in a primary classroom*. New York: Teachers College Press.

Gerber, M., & Johnson, A. (1998). *Your self-confident baby*. New York: John Wiley.

Gonzalez-Mena, J. (1993). *Multicultural issues in child care*. Mountain View, CA: Mayfield.

Gonzalez-Mena, J., & Eyer, D.W. (1989). *Infants, toddlers, and caregivers*. Mountain View, CA: Mayfield.

Goudge, E. (1948). *Pilgrim's Inn*. New York: Coward-McCann.

Gronlund, G. (1992). Ninja Turtle play in my kindergarten classroom. *Young Children, 48*(1), 21–25.

Jones, E. (1961). Communication: By word or deed? *Journal of Nursery Education, 17*(1), 7–8.

Jones, E. (Ed.) (1983). *On the growing edge: College teachers making changes*. Pasadena, CA: Pacific Oaks College.

Jones, E. (1986). *Teaching adults: An active learning approach*. Washington, DC: National Association for the Education of Young Children.

Jones, E. (Ed.). (1993). *Growing teachers: Partnerships in staff development*. Washington, DC: National Association for the Education of Young Children.

Jones, E. (2003). Playing to get smart. *Young Children, 58*(3), 32–36.

Jones, E., Evans, K., & Rencken, K. S. (2001). *The lively kindergarten: Emergent curriculum in action*. Washington, DC: National Association for the Education of Young Children.

Jones, E., & Nimmo, J. (1994). *Emergent curriculum*. Washington, DC: National Association for the Education of Young Children.

Jones, E., & Nimmo, J. (1999). Collaboration, conflict and change: Thoughts on education as provocation. *Young Children, 54*(1), 5–10.

Jones, E., & Prescott, E. (1984). *Dimensions of teaching-learning environments: A handbook for teachers in elementary schools and day care centers*. Pasadena, CA: Pacific Oaks College.

Jones, E., & Reynolds, G. (1992). *The play's the thing: Teachers' roles in children's play*. New York: Teachers College Press.

Kamii, C. (1982). Autonomy as the aim of education: Implications of Piaget's theory. Appendix to *Number in preschool and kindergarten*. Washington, DC: National Association for the Education of Young Children.

Kamii, C. (1985). Leading primary education toward excellence: Beyond worksheets and drill. *Young Children, 40*(6), 3–9.

Katz, L. G. (1993) A national goals wish list. *Young Children, 48*(3), 2.

Kipling, R. (1978). *Just so stories*. New York: Weathervane Books. (Original work published 1902)

LaFlamme, M. (n.d.). *Playing with ideas: A guidebook for teachers who enjoy thinking with children*. Albuquerque: University of New Mexico Family Development Program.

Magee, J., & Jones, E. (2004). Leave no grown-up behind: Coming to terms with technology. *Young Children, 59*(3), 13–20.

McCullough, C. (1977). *The Thorn Birds*. New York: Harper & Row.

Minarik, E. H. (1957). *Little Bear*. New York: Harper.

Moore, K. (1998). *Extending experience: John Dewey, intercommunication, and conversation in the early childhood classroom*. Unpublished master's thesis, Pacific Oaks College, Pasadena, CA.

Noddings, N. (1992). *The challenge to care in schools: An alternative approach to education*. New York: Teachers College Press.

Paley, V. (1988). *Bad guys don't have birthdays: Fantasy play at four*. Chicago: University of Chicago Press.

Piaget, J. (1951). *Play, dreams, and imitation in childhood*. New York: Norton.

Piaget, J. (1973) *To understand is to invent*. New York: Grossman.

Piper, G. (2005). *Loner as home visitor*. Unpublished master's thesis, Pacific Oaks College, Pasadena, CA.

Read, L. (1993). *Finding the family in family grouping: Pro-social behaviors in a mixed-age classroom*. Unpublished master's thesis, Pacific Oaks College, Pasadena, CA.

Reagon, B. J. (1983). Coalition politics: Turning the century. In B. Smith (Ed.), *Home girls: A Black feminist anthology* (pp. 356–368). New York: Kitchen Table, Women of Color Press.

Reynolds, G., & Jones, E. (1997). *Master players: Learning from children at play*. New York: Teachers College Press.

Sarason, S. B. (1972). *The creation of settings and the future societies*. San Francisco: Jossey-Bass.

Scudder, M. E. D. (1978). *Feelings: An integral part of the curriculum*. (Occasional Paper). Pacific Oaks College, Pasadena, CA.

Silko, L. M. (1977). *Ceremony*. New York: Viking Penguin.

Steinman, L. (2004, May 16). Book/lecture review of James Hillman, *A terrible love of war*. *Los Angeles Times*, p. E4.

Truss, L. (2003). *Eats, shoots and leaves: The zero tolerance approach to punctuation*. London: Profile Books.

United Nations (1959). *Declaration of the rights of the child.* http://www.unhcrh.ch/
    html/menu3/b/25.htm

Vygotsky, L. S. (1978). *Mind in society: The development of higher psychological pro-
    cesses.* Cambridge: Harvard University Press.

Wasserman, S. (2000). *Serious players in the primary classroom: Empowering chil-
    dren through active learning experiences* (2nd ed.). New York: Teachers Col-
    lege Press.

Index

About the Authors

ELIZABETH JONES is a member of the faculty in Human Development at Pacific Oaks College and Children's School in Pasadena, California, where she has taught both adults and children. She earned an M.A. in child development at the University of Wisconsin and a Ph.D. in sociology at the University of Southern California. She is author of numerous articles and books, including *The Play's the Thing* (1992) and *Master Players* (1997) with Gretchen Reynolds, *Growing Teachers* (1993), *Emergent Curriculum* (1994) with John Nimmo, and *The Lively Kindergarten* (2001) with Kathleen Evans and Kay Rencken.

RENATTA M. COOPER is the Education Coordinator for the Los Angeles County Office of Child Care, and a Commissioner for First 5 LA. She earned a B.A. in early childhood education and a teaching credential at Towson State University, as well as an M.A. in human development at Pacific Oaks College. She is a board member of the national organization Playing for Keeps. Formerly a faculty member of Pacific Oaks College, she served as Director of the Infant/Toddler/Parent program in Pacific Oaks Children's School, and later as Director of the Jones/Prescott Institute. She is author of numerous articles, and this is her first book.